By Choice

THE UNCONVENTIONAL STORY OF

JOSE THOMAS

By Choice

VINOD MATHEW

HARPER
VANTAGE

First published in India by Harper Vantage 2023
An imprint of HarperCollins *Publishers*
4th Floor, Tower A, Building No. 10, DLF Cyber City,
DLF Phase II, Gurugram, Haryana – 122002
www.harpercollins.co.in

2 4 6 8 10 9 7 5 3 1

P-ISBN: 978-93-5699-389-1
E-ISBN: 978-93-5699-388-4

Typeset in 11.5/15.2 Berling LT Std at
Manipal Technologies Limited, Manipal

Printed and bound at
Thomson Press (India) Ltd.

To my parents—A. M. Chacko and Aleyamma Chacko

CONTENTS

FOREWORD

JT: An Enigma

MY ASSOCIATION WITH JOSE THOMAS BEGAN A FEW YEARS ago when I met him while we were shooting for film *Twenty-20* in which I played the lead role. The location for the film shoot belonged to Jose and I was given to understand that he had granted permission for the shoot only because I was the protagonist. I had heard of him but had never met him until then and this meeting marked the beginning of a long and cherished friendship.

Jose Thomas is fondly referred to as 'JT' by people who know him. As our friendship blossomed, we discovered quite a few common interests, especially our love for the arts, food and travel. Being an avid globetrotter, my many travels with JT have always been lovely experiences. Many of these experiences during our travels have been narrated by JT in this book.

JT is passionate about the arts. He not only sings well but also plays the drums superbly. He has a set up in his house in New York where budding artists get together for jamming sessions. He has set up the Jose Thomas Performing Arts Centre (JT PAC) in Kochi, Kerala—an avant-garde performing arts centre that has hosted and continues to host major events. It is a solid testimony to JT's passion for the arts.

As a devout family man, JT travels with his family often and spends quality time with them. He loves to cook for his family whenever an opportunity arises and I have also joined him on many occasions, donning the chef's hat! He is also an avid aviation enthusiast—a passion that has been captured in this book.

JT comes across to me as a resilient, dynamic, street-smart person with enormous courage. He has diversified business interests and has built the 'Choice' brand, initiated by his late father into a mega conglomerate today in the fields of education, food, shipping, etc. A disciplined businessman, he has instilled this trait in his children, who will no doubt carry on this legacy. Jose's wife, Elizabeth, is a pillar of strength for the family and the way she manages Jose's idiosyncrasies is admirable.

JT is also somewhat of an enigma to me. He is a warm personality, yet he is slow in cultivating friendships and has only a few close friends. I, for one, do know that if the first barrier is crossed, JT is really a very charming, warm and irresistible friend. We have mutual respect and admiration for each other and share a friendship that is pure and pristine, without any expectations of each other. This allows us to laugh, crack jokes and ridicule each other whenever we meet. Every time we get together, it is a celebration. I pray that the Almighty continues to bless JT and his family with prosperity and peace.

As I read this book, written in an extraordinarily beautiful way by Vinod Mathew, I realized that JT is a far more dynamic personality than the one I had perceived him to be. The kind of risks he has taken and the kind of challenges he has faced reveal a dual personality in JT—there is a Jose Thomas I know and the evolved JT that I confess I did not know. That is, at least, not until now.

Mohanlal,
Actor, Malayalam film industry

A NOTE FROM THE AUTHOR

WRITING THE TRUE STORY OF A LIVING MAN IS NOT AMONG the easiest of tasks. I have spent equal amounts of time over a period of thirty years between financial and mainstream journalism. So why did I construct an entire book around a person who, at the best of times, wears his quirky persona label like a badge of honour?

As I started spending time with Jose Thomas over a year ago, we both knew where it was eventually headed. Yet, it took a while for both of us to get going with the project. He kept saying it would be too bold on his part to assume that his life's journey was worth putting down on paper. I felt unsure whether he would tolerate my style of journalistic writing.

This went on for a while before he said something that grabbed my attention. When he said nonchalantly, 'My story is more about failures than successes', I was truly hooked.

Here was a man with many shades of grey about him, one who was willing to discuss his shortfalls and inadequacies. Sure, he would get uneasy while discussing his many flaws, some of them leading his company to the brink of collapse, but the fact remained that he was ready to have them put in the public domain.

If accumulation of wealth was the criterion, then there were many from his own town who were far wealthier and had arrived as corporate entities in their own right. However, what swung my attention in JT's favour was the undeniable fact that his life was far more eventful and colourful. It boasted of a multitude of adventures not experienced by many of his peers. He always claimed to be in a different league. Consider the contents of this book an exhaustive verification of his claims.

Also portrayed here are some of the mundane, perplexing setbacks that many people face during their lifetime. The attempt here is to juxtapose situations that not many would be brave enough to acknowledge—let alone allow them to be chronicled in a biography. In that sense, this is a handbook for those who want to pursue their dreams and live life on their own terms in face of life-altering situations.

This book is essentially based on the information shared by Jose Thomas. While a fact check has been done on the verifiable events, there are quite a few instances that appear as minor ingredients or garnishing in a recipe. Inaccuracies, if any, in the reconstruction of a situation are inadvertent.

To make this narration factually accurate, the protagonist was required to delve into the past and articulate some eventful episodes of his life. Sometimes it was fun—to get Jose Thomas to walk back in time and relive those incidents. There were occasions when he would develop a mental block and show reluctance about sharing details. For example, during those Zoom calls from New Jersey, I would ask him details about those critical days he was stationed in Delhi and how Choice Air missed out on the Air Taxi licence.

He enjoyed the advantage of being able to disconnect, saying he was too tired, or with the words, 'Let us call it a day!' Often, he would put off the topic for the following day and when reminded, he would say 'Why are you spoiling my evening, asking me to relive those dark days?' It would take multiple interactions before I could get the full picture, often with supplementary inputs from his former associates.

I suspect it often had a cathartic effect on him. It is never an easy task to relive one's spectacular failures. This was true for Jose as well, despite the fact that the stated purpose behind writing this book was to tackle successes and failures with an even hand.

Add to that the technical hurdles of cross-verifying dates, names of people from many decades ago and our plate was full.

It was even more laborious to get him to answer questions in the written form. The questions raised with supplementary add-ons would run into neat paragraphs. Invariably, the response by mail would have monosyllabic answers—'Yes', 'No', 'Forgot'. But there were also occasions when he would wax eloquent on his adventures. Then the challenge would be to get him to stop, convincing him that such anecdotes were outside the scope of this book.

His refrain has been—and I suspect would continue to be—that he has disclosed not more than 50 per cent of his life's experiences, as if holding out gave him some kind of quirky pleasure. When we started out, it was more like 'You don't know even 30 per cent of what I have been through'. By that calculation, this book captures only about 20 per cent of his stories.

The good thing here is he is not overtly shy of narrating his many setbacks, something many others would brush under the narrative carpet. So, did he work towards those outcomes or were they impulsive decisions? In many cases, it was a combination of both. Perhaps that is what sets him apart from the rest of the corporate pack and makes this book worth reading.

An element that runs throughout the book—sometimes in a linear manner, on occasions in elliptical orbits—and puts many situations in perspective is his dual personas, Jose and JT. It was one of his nephews who first started calling him JT, maybe he felt calling him uncle in office was not an option. Over the years, he got accustomed to being addressed by his initials. Soon, it began to assume deeper implications—it got entrenched in his character.

It goes beyond young Jose growing up and taking on the tag of JT as he started doing well. While JT is polished, sophisticated, not prone to risks, young Jose rarely thinks twice before going on wild goose chases and taking enormous risks.

This is how Jose Thomas puts it in perspective: 'For a good part of my life, whenever I took up high-risk projects, I often felt I was no longer in control. It was as if my father, the unknown hero of my life, whose approval I never got, began to take control of many of the decisions I made. Soon, I began taking up difficult tasks so that my father would acknowledge my achievements.'

As Jose went out on a limb to seek out opportunities that did not fit the 'ordinary', he found it increasingly difficult to justify his actions to his family and associates. Thus, Jose would take custody of an abandoned ship, quell a near-rebellion by the crew, dispense with their services, get the cargo loaded onto other vessels, sail all the way to Sudan and earn his first windfall.

By his own admission, the struggle for supremacy between Jose, the person he used to be, and JT, the person he grew up to become, will not get resolved till the day he dies. One has to read the epilogue of this book to fully comprehend what he means by that. The identity of JT began as a branding tool but soon it consumed his personality.

This book attempts to chronicle what went into the making of some of his ventures, and why a few of them turned into misadventures. It is for the reader to decide whether the colourful palettes painted by Jose, on behalf of JT, were 'by choice'.

PROLOGUE

The Maverick of the East

THIS IS THE TALE OF A YOUNG BOY WHO LOVED TO DREAM. He would gaze across the sea from the shores of his hometown in Kochi and be amazed by the ships that came calling at the Cochin port in Willingdon Island. He dreamt of mastering the seas and engaging with those ships for commercial gain. Much to the dismay of those around, as Jose grew older, not only did his dreams get bigger and bolder, he began trying to live out those dreams.

Soon, he began exhorting those around him to join him in the pursuit of these goals. The swelling ranks of his employees, which probably comprised many non-believers, went along with him on these adventures. Yet, his peers in the trading community were in no doubt that he was consumed by delusions of grandeur. Some found traits of Don Quixote in him, minus of course his trusted Sancho Panza, since Jose was a loner.

They also made snide remarks about his lavish partying culture right through the years, convinced he was a show-off. They could not fathom why he 'wasted money' by entertaining friends, even strangers who turned up to share their dreams with him. The 'King of Good Times' label was already bestowed on Vijay Mallya. Otherwise, they would have thrust it upon Jose!

Jose, however, was as unfazed by the criticism as he was by the failures that sometimes came his way. The stoic fortitude with which he tackled the disappointments from his boyhood days seemed to come in handy when many of his well-conceived plans stumbled for incomprehensible reasons.

In his own words, he would have sunk under the turbulence that rocked his mainline revenue options had he not decided to keep his foot in more than one boat at a time. He was never quite the alchemist of success, as his experiments often turned volatile and scalded many.

Jose reiterates that each of his life-altering step was an act of choice. From salvaging an abandoned ship and taking the cargo all the way to Khartoum, Sudan, in the early 1980s, or taking a chance to start his own business in the US, to joining hands with a European settled in Zimbabwe to start a $50 million shrimp-processing plant in Mozambique, he has always *chosen* the path he would tread. Inevitably, the will of Jose would try to impose upon the acquired persona of JT and vice versa.

So, was it Jose or JT who went all out, throwing all his cards on the table while trying to start an airline? During the recent pandemic, was it JT or Jose who sailed his yacht along the Eastern Seaboard, still nurturing his youthful dream of operating a shipping line where the Choice insignia fluttered in the wind?

Jose is not blind to a major chink in his armour that has often kept his Group at a constant disadvantage—his penchant for doing everything himself. He says he holds himself up to such an impossibly high standard that his team does not measure up to it. His critics swear his growth has been in fits and starts only on account of his unease with delegating work. There are shades of truth in both arguments.

Jose sums it up as only he can: 'Choice is my friend, my enemy, my companion, my conscience, my passion, my preoccupation, my driving force and my all-consuming fear. Each thing I do, ventures I undertake, is in pursuit of this dream. It has one name, one voice, one mantra—Choice.'

1

GILLETTE JOSE

A YOUNG BOY IN HIS EARLY TEENS GOT SHIPPED OUT FROM his native town, Kochi, to Nirmala School in the Idukki district as a resident student. He was pretty much removed from his comfort zone, forced to share his living quarters with a bunch of rich children. Soon enough, he started feeling left out, as hard cash—the magic wand that would get him entrenched with the rest in the boarding—was difficult to come by. Result: young Jose soon began to feel lonely.

All the boarding school students used to be taken to a nearby chapel. After the church service there, they would watch the bidding process of agricultural products, even poultry by the laity. The church would discreetly allow its premises to be turned into a platform for buying and selling goods, with the proceeds going to the church. It was a commercial activity, no doubt, but done with the purpose of augmenting the church revenue.

That got young Jose to come out of his sullen mood and avidly watch the proceedings. An idea began taking shape in his imaginative mind. Aiming for a piece of the action, he started puzzling over a plan to make this happen. Later, during one of his monthly trips home, he chanced upon Mr Koya—who used to supply foreign goods from ships calling at the port—selling foreign liquor and toiletries, to the elite of the city, including Jose's dad.

Those were the days when all kinds of imported goods were perceived as an indulgence as they broadly came under the contraband label. It was a phase during post-Independence coming-of-age era in India when only home-grown brands were available, right from cosmetics to automobiles. The untold reality was that there was an acute scarcity of foreign exchange, more than any love for desi goods.

To give it perspective, the antipathy towards foreign goods began garnering such political mileage that by 1974, Prime Minister Indira Gandhi would ban Coca Cola in India. This state of affairs would continue till the early 1990s when the economy was finally opened up as the liberalization era began during the tenure of Manmohan Singh as finance minister.*

For young Jose, the intricacies of foreign exchange were of little concern. His line of thinking was pretty straightforward—he had to find a way to establish himself as a worthy candidate for the unfaltering attention of his fellow boarders who had so far ignored him and even snubbed him. He befriended Koya with one thing in mind—finding out what all variety of goods were in his box.

There were imported liquor bottles, cartons of cigarettes and a whole lot of other interesting goods. However, all that did not interest him. He identified bundles of Gillette blades

---

* Deepak Nayyar '1991: Economic liberalization and political process', Live Mint, 13 October 2016, https://www.livemint.com/Opinion/l46jd4x7sEnYgxizMcnq3M/1991-economic-liberalization-and-political-process.html

as something that could be sold in the church premises. He then persuaded Koya to part with a few dozen packets on credit, against the promise of a 20 per cent higher price than what he got in Kochi. He convinced Koya to agree to a thirty-day credit which was quite a feat. In the world of finance, this is called extended credit.

It took some serious convincing to get a reluctant Koya to agree as he was only too aware that there was no guarantee that his blades could be sold by the young boy or if he would earn a profit as he claimed. But the deed was done and a gleeful Jose took delivery of his first consignment, with only his promise offered as a bill of sale.

The following Sunday, after the mass, the school parish church witnessed a strange sight. A string of well-heeled adults making a beeline for the shade of a nearby tree, leaving their wives to handle the routine bidding and loading of goods into their cars. Holding centre-stage was a confident young Jose, with a bundle of Gillette blade packets, spread out before him, negotiating rates with his customers. It was a clandestine operation as he had to conduct the business right under the nose of his teachers, without drawing their attention to what was happening.

Not only did he sell at more than double his buying price, but he also made solicitous inquiries about other foreign toiletry products they were looking to buy. That day marked the birth of a nascent young entrepreneur. He had locked all the three ingredients necessary to conduct business—a good product, a market to sell it, and potential buyers with cash to spare.

Even more significantly, he had managed to get a line of credit from his supplier and he ended the day with a handsome profit. For 'Gillette Jose', as he would come to be known in that locality for many years, this was merely the beginning. The year was 1968; Jose had made a grand entry into the teenage club.

His nose for potential opportunities that began to be honed with the Gillette blade episode would continue to be his ally right through his life. Thus began the incredible journey of a precocious young boy who declared to the world his business prowess even before hitting his teens. Each milestone defines the evolution of the youngster into a different genre of entrepreneurship, far removed from that of his peer group.

After finishing his studies from Nirmala School, Muvattupuzha, it was with a sense of relief that Jose took admission into his pre-degree course in St Albert's College, Kochi. As he began his adolescent journey in a typical college campus in Kerala, academics was perhaps not the priority. It was more about setting out on a voyage of self-discovery, where young boys and girls in their teens mingled, new friendships sprang up, and in many cases—love blossomed.

So it did for Jose, though it took his sister—studying at another college—to get his love life going. In an effort to see him come out of his shell, she got one of her friends to send him messages. He began to respond, but soon things turned serious between them, which was not what his sister desired. So she got another mate of hers to befriend him.

The second friendship that Jose got into took an even more serious turn as they truly fell in love. The matter reached his mother's ears and she gave him an a tough choice: it was either the relationship or getting involved in the family business. Jose says he was forced to give up his first love. But the girl, he came to know later, felt he had chosen Choice over her.

Thus ended his first love and he convinced himself that he could never afford to be in a similar position again. Thereafter, he lost no time in putting in a few hours each day at the Coronation Club near his house in Mattancherry, playing badminton. As luck would have it, many Gujarati merchants who monopolized the spice trade in Kerala used to frequent the club. That is where Jose met Shafi, who was a prominent commodity trader in Mattancherry. His regular interactions with Shafi fuelled his interest in commodity trade.

Soon, they were weighing the options on Jose turning into a supplier of betel nut, one of the many commodities Shafi traded in. Perhaps Shafi wanted a fresh line of supply, so he vetted the youngster's appetite for becoming an entrepreneur. At the same time, the hunger in Jose to get engaged in some kind of activity was there for all to see. When Shafi explained to him how to go about procuring betel nut and selling it at a profit, Jose took the plunge.

He was on cloud nine each time he sighted large volumes of betel nut on the trees; he was mentally counting the money that he was going to make out of the deal. Just as his college mates were fully immersed in campus life, which, especially in Kerala, is mostly about student politics and tedious courtships that take years to fructify, young Jose began taking the Ernakulam–Pala route by bus to scope out the availability of the raw material.

Thus, he had identified the commodity as also the market. All that was left to do was procure the commodity. His confidence level was so high, exuberance so infectious that no thought was spared for his inexperience. It was his moment of truth as a trader in the making.

Across the hilly terrain of Kanjirapally in Kottayam district, he had already spotted hundreds of betel nut trees, many of them along the expansive grounds of his sister-in-law's ancestral house. He knew he could convince her to lay his hands on the betel nut, especially with his mother backing his maiden effort to emerge as a commodity trader. Not only his mother, his sisters too were rooting for him, even as his father was perhaps unaware, at best somewhat sceptical. Many farm holdings in the nearby Pala region had vast betel nut cultivation.

The money to buy the nuts was procured from his mother, with the promise that he would return it with interest once he got paid by the Gujarati merchants. As he returned from each trip with sack loads of betel nut, his mother, sisters, also a few housemaids, chipped in by crack-drying the betel nut in the night and the ensuing days.

There was a sense of excitement in the family circles as young Jose was successfully making his presence felt in the world of business, showing immense promise so early in his life. His sisters constantly prayed for his success, as they planned the purchase of cosmetics and toiletries from the money he would share from the profits.

Even as betel nut, a few kilos each time, began finding its way into the courtyard of his house, young Jose widened his raw material procurement to include the distant Malabar region, famous for its higher yield and better price. His bus journeys started getting rerouted to Malappuram district.

While identifying fresh grounds with good betel nut yield, Jose began submitting his name for any inter-school competitions in those areas. At home, as everyone knew the real story, they looked on indulgently as the young scion of the family was cutting his teeth as an entrepreneur.

No surprise then as here was an adolescent willing to give up his leisure time to pursue his entrepreneurial dreams with a rare determination. By then, Jose had accumulated ten sackloads of betel nut, all purchased with money raised from those who wanted a share in the proceeds.

The total amount thus borrowed for betel nut procurement stood at ₹5,000. That was hardly a matter for worry as the rates which he had from Shafi before he set out on the venture, would easily net him ₹12,000, more than double his invested money. Sleep deserted Jose as he kept awake during the night, relishing the fat profit he was about to make.

When the D-day arrived, he loaded the dried betel nut before heading out to Shafi's shop. He was mentally calculating how much he would give to his mother and sisters after returning the borrowed capital. He was unprepared for the bombshell that was soon to be dropped on him. Shafi, till then his well-wisher, suddenly turned all business-like, pointing out how raw the betel nut load was, not properly dried and therefore not acceptable for commercial use.

It was a catastrophe. Jose would realize in the days to come that he had failed the quality control test for the first time. He sold the entire batch for ₹1,500. The net loss was ₹3,500, closer to ₹4,000 considering transportation expenses. A harsh lesson was learned quite early in his life. If anything, the setback only strengthened his resolve to establish himself as a trader.

His connections with the Mattancherry merchant community would come to his aid a few years down the line when he will need to procure cargo for the Red Sea region on behalf of Maldives Shipping.

Thus began his push into the commodity market, getting familiar with 'forward contracts' and 'spot auctions'. He leveraged these lessons.

2

KLE 5382

IN 1972, JOSE WAS A DAY SCHOLAR AT ST ALBERT'S COLLEGE, Banerjee Road. Being the tenth-born in a crowded household of eleven children brought with it the burden of being unheard and unseen. For an impatient seventeen-year-old, determined to prove to his father that it was he, of his three sons and eight daughters who was the true successor, the going could only have been doubly difficult.

Thus, the Gillette blade episode and later on the commodity trading effort were all as much part of his unbridled anxiety to draw his father's attention to his budding prowess as they were frantic attempts to communicate with his father. Perhaps the only person who realized what young Jose was up to was his mother, Annamma Thomas.

It was but natural that she would remain his strongest ally later on when the family business faced its first severe test in 1976 and his eldest brother, O.T. Alexander, opted to part with the mother company by setting up his venture, National Seafood. Hence, a good part of his life as a teenager was spent with the primary goal of impressing his father.

To a youngster, it was like trying to move mountains. But he never gave up hope. He knew his father's penchant to present an inscrutable countenance that showed very little of what he felt. So, Jose would gauge his response to some of his ventures through his mother. Between late 1971 and early 1972, Jose had started frequenting the Choice Canning factory. He would try suggesting improvements, only to be shooed away by the managers. The craving to be recognized kept gnawing away at Jose.

The breakthrough came in the second half of 1972, after a few failed attempts by him to convince the managers at the Kannamaly factory. His theory was that the many trucks used to carry prawns to the factory and later to the harbour were not cost-effective as they all had petrol engines. He decided to take the argument to his father, once again using his mother as an intermediary.

According to Jose (this is what he would like to believe), his father agreed to convert one truck to diesel because he saw a spark in the youngster that reminded his father of what he used to be as a youngster. The moment his father agreed to test out his theory of saving on fuel cost by replacing the petrol engine of one of the Bedford trucks with a diesel engine, Jose realized he had joined the race after all, because the head of the family had finally started to take notice of his tenth offspring. The truck chosen bore the licence plate KLE 5382.

Even in those days, Kunnamkulam was the one-stop destination for anyone looking for second-hand automobile parts, including diesel engines. That is where Jose, accompanied by his brother Tom, went, stayed at a lodge, and started searching for the engine. They got it for a tidy sum of ₹6,000 and headed back to the Popular Automobiles, Shanmugham Road outlet, where the engine of KLE 5382 was to be modified under the supervision of Jose.

But a sudden illness started plaguing his father. Soon, it began getting difficult for Jose to find time to be at the workshop where the vehicle was undergoing the engine makeover. Jose still remembers those traumatic days.

'My father unexpectedly fell ill towards the second half of September 1972. It was perhaps the first time in my memory that I saw my father not in control of things. Nobody knew what to make of it as the decision-maker had become a non-participant in the process. Elders in the family and his friends decided to rush him to Lisie Hospital,' says Jose.

'The walls of the hospital room where my father was admitted started reverberating with prayers, easily more prayers than one would hear in a church. The following day my father was taken for a battery of investigations, many of them invasive. He was poked with needles and scalpels for body fluids and samples. Even then, none of us had a sense that anything was seriously amiss. After all, it was only a check-up,' he adds.

The very next day, the doctors decided he needed to be operated on. The surgery perplexed the family as it was a little too sudden. The tests revealed that O.C. Thomas had lung cancer. The surgery took place the next day, but it was unsuccessful as the lumps could not be completely removed.

'Even while in the ICU, my father kept enquiring about the market value of the goods, mainly prawns, its purchase and shipping details. The spirited man that he was, his mind remained tuned in on Choice. Soon, I realized the surgery was only a last-ditch effort to save his life. I am still wracked by the memories of how my father was worried more about his incomplete work and unfinished plans than his fast deteriorating health condition,' remembers Jose.

As Jose kept rushing between the hospital and the workshop, he knew there was not much time to accomplish the one deed that had his ailing father's approval. What was to be his hour of recognition from his father for a job well done got lost in a panic-stricken household faced with the tragedy of the patriarch fighting a losing battle with time.

On 3 October 1972, the head of the family and one of the founders of Choice Canning Company, Olassayil Chandy Thomas passed away. From the day he was taken to the hospital, he had lasted barely a week. A mighty tree had fallen. Jose was shattered. The final chance to get his father to appreciate his true worth was lost. All efforts to transform KLE 5382 and get the company to cut its costs, could never be appreciated by his father.

All he yearned for was a pat on his shoulder, a glance of appreciation, a smile of encouragement. That was not to be with the unfortunate turn of events. It was hardly a solace for him that his father's final journey to his last resting place, the funeral procession, was on KLE 5382, which had undergone a makeover not with this purpose in mind.

It hurt Jose as much as made him proud in a warped sense that his father even after his death did find some use for the refurbished KLE 5382. He was left with a deep personal wound, one that refused to heal. Regrets about the personal time that he never had with his father would haunt him forever.

There were the many conversations that they never had, which could now be only played out over and over again in his mind. In the years to come, he would in the recesses of his mind seek his father's approval at every critical stage. Each milestone for the Choice Group would be a dedication to the legend that was O.C. Thomas. His father's untimely death literally played havoc with the Olassayil family.

The relatives and associates paid their respects. The family continued to remain numb. The big question facing the family was 'What next?' Suggestions came thick and fast, some were unassuming and helpful, others disruptive.

'My eldest brother Alex's wife belonged to the renowned Puthenangady family in Kanjirapally. Her father advised that we all leave for Kanjirapally. The logic was that Choice would now be difficult to run with his partners either wanting control or moving out. He vowed to take care of all of us. I was mortified when my elder siblings, lacking in foresight, quietly nodded their heads in agreement,' he recalls.

That marked the birth of the rebel son, the one who opposed this plan tooth and nail, talking back to the head of his family. Heated words were exchanged. Luckily for Jose, his mother came out in his support. The plan to salvage the fortunes of the Olassayil family by getting them to relocate to Kanjirapally had to be dropped.

The seeds of discord had been sown! The rebellious streak in Jose would only grow over the next couple of years. At the receiving end would be renowned names, including MNCs that would get to know the rebel was also stubborn. Jose would keep going till he resolved the issue to his satisfaction.

He would choose the path less taken and pursue the most difficult assignments. Some would call it living on the knife's edge. Jose understood only too well that that alone would get him into the big league. This wild streak in him reached a crescendo when he hit his thirties.

His penchant to go berserk in pursuit of a pricey goal with no assured guarantee of success would peter out over the years, as he began to take pride in wearing a more sober hat. The wild spirit in him still rears its head now and then, filling his life story with the kind of action one rarely finds in other men. Yet, Jose would find plausible explanations to justify his typical manner of pursuing success.

3

THE FIERCE MATRIARCH

O.C. THOMAS WAS AMONG THE FOUNDING MEMBERS OF Choice Canning Company in November 1962 as a partnership firm along with R. Madhavan Nayar, joined later by P.K. Nair. Once the latter passed away, the partnership was limited to Nayar and Thomas. Begun with twenty-five employees for exporting processed canned shrimp, Choice Canning went on to set up a modern block-frozen shrimp factory at Kannamaly in 1969.

The untimely passing of O.C. Thomas at the age of sixty was soon to set in motion a chain of events initially precipitated by the exit of his two partners, leaving the eldest son, Alexander, to take it forward as a family-owned enterprise. Initially, everything seemed fine as the eldest son took over the reins, supported by his mother and two brothers. However, with the departure of the original partners, there also came a slew of financial woes.

The Bank of India froze the company accounts as the ownership changed hands quite suddenly and, for a brief period, the Choice Canning Company remained shut. The main source of revenue then was from selling coconuts from the land the family possessed, where the yield was not less than 50,000 coconuts at each harvest.

What transpired during the days that followed, how the Choice Group came into the Olassayil family with origins in the mid-Travancore town of Changanassery, is narrated below by Venugopal C. Govind,* who played a mediator's role:

When I first met Jose with his father, he was a young man in his teens. I was impressed with this bright effervescent young lad who displayed dynamism and ambition. His father was the working partner looking after the business affairs of Choice Canning Company, a marine product canning and exporting unit set up as per the articles of partnership.

The majority shares were held by the late R. Madhavan Nayar, who was the pioneer in the seafood processing and exports industry in India. They were the clients of Messers Varma & Varma Chartered Accountants, where I later became managing partner. We were the auditors and tax consultants of Choice Canning Company. O.C. Thomas, or OC, as he was fondly called, was a very hard-working businessman.

Since Madhavan Nayar had his own large seafood processing and exporting company, he had entrusted the management of Choice Canning Company almost entirely to OC, who was managing the company quite efficiently. As the business grew, Nayar inducted P.K. Nair, a retired corporate executive, who was the younger brother of Justice P. Govindan Nair of the Kerala High Court, as a full-time partner of the firm.

---

* Venugopal C. Govind, chartered accountant, auditor, managing partner of Varma & Varma, has played a major role in structuring corporate succession plans. The Choice Group as it is known today, came into existence following his mediation in the 1970s.

A couple of years later, Nair expired. Once again, the full responsibility of managing the firm fell on OC, who had by then become seasoned in handling the entire factory. But the seafood industry as a whole started facing fresh challenges. The strain was beginning to bear upon OC.

It was a shock when he passed away in 1972, at the relatively young age of sixty, leaving behind his wife who was barely fifty, seven daughters and three sons. O.T. Alexander, the eldest son, had joined his father in business a couple of years ago after his graduation. The second son, Tom, and the youngest, Jose, had not finished their education.

Alex, though he did not have much business exposure, was a fast learner. Tom was unassuming and willing to take up whatever responsibility that came his way. Jose, probably still a teenager, was dynamic and highly ambitious. Alex started establishing himself and steering the business fairly satisfactorily, with guidance from Nayar. Nearly two years thus passed without any major upheavals.

By then, Jose was brimming with enthusiasm and wanted to enter the business. Alex too felt it made sense to let him join the business. Jose was put in charge of the firm's operations in Madras.

To his dismay, Jose's innovative efforts did not succeed. Operational profits gave way to losses. It was then decided to apply the brakes in Madras and the youngster was asked to shift his base to Kochi. Choice Canning Company was also hit by the general slide in the seafood industry. Nayar was beginning to get concerned about how to deal with the difficult scenario and challenges. He shared his concern with Alex, who was in charge of day-to-day operations.

One day Annamma dropped in at my office. I was meeting her for the first time and was deeply impressed by her poise, dignity and most importantly her air of self-confidence. She started narrating how her husband spent all of his productive years working for the firm, how passionate was his attachment to the firm which he always dreamt and spoke of developing amidst the most difficult challenges. She underlined how he had struggled to bring the firm to its present level.

She said had her husband lived longer, he would certainly have taken the firm to greater heights. She then paused for a while and said, 'We have only this firm for us and we would like to keep it.' I was a bit surprised at this sudden statement, but then she clarified, 'You must be wondering what I am talking about. If you could request Madhavan Nayar sir to hand over the firm to us, we will ensure that my sons will run the firm well.'

I looked at her in disbelief and asked, 'Do you think your sons could run this firm all by themselves? They are too young and don't yet have sufficient experience in this highly competitive processing and export environment.'

With a confident smile, she said, 'Yes, sure. I have thought over it for several weeks now. They will learn to manage.'

I did not disagree but told her in all seriousness that this firm substantially belonged to Nayar. I was unsure whether he would agree to dispose of it now, even if it was to his former partner's family.

I asked, 'Are you now in a financial position to buy him out?'

She answered innocently, but bluntly, 'We don't have much to give him now. For sure, we will pay him in instalments, if he would allow that.'

I was amazed, to say the least, the first steps of corporate negotiation came from an elderly housewife and a mother, who wanted to get control of the company for her young children! I knew that the idea was not easily workable and a seasoned professional like Nayar would not dispose of his interest in the firm so easily.

I told her that I was not sure that her proposal would get approved. Nevertheless, I agreed to talk to Nayar and get back to her in a few days. Annamma got up saying, 'You have to do this for us. I shall come again to discuss this.' That was how our first meeting ended. The interview left me with mixed feelings.

I was deeply impressed by the lady who showed steely determination to do right by her children, her vision and willpower. After a few days, I presented the proposal to Nayar. He heard me out and asked me in a low tone, 'Do you think this is feasible?'

I had no immediate answer for him in my professional capacity. I knew he already had long-term plans for the firm. All I said was, 'If you think they need to be helped, there could be a way forward.' After close to an hour of discussions covering all aspects of the matter, he wound up our meeting, saying, 'Thomas was good, I would certainly want to help, but as to how this can be done, let us think.'

After another meeting with Nayar, it was agreed that he would hand over his share in the firm to the family at a fair, reasonable consideration which the Thomas family could afford. More crucial was the decision by Nayar to allow them to pay him the amount in instalments.

My next meeting with Annamma was quite formal. I tried to drive home three points, to caution her about the possible pitfalls of pursuing her request. First, there was tremendous risk in seafood exports, the weight of which would be borne by her young sons, none with enough experience in the industry. Secondly, they would be shutting out a good opportunity to receive a substantial sum as a one-time settlement which they would get if they were to surrender their share to Nayar, one that I would negotiate on their behalf. Finally, and most importantly, the financial burden on the family, if Nayar did agree to hand over Choice Canning, would prove to be heavy. This would last for a long period.

There was no change in her firm stand. She said with a sense of reassurance that each of her sons had different qualities. She said, 'Alex is competent and mature, already with some experience. Tom is hard-working while Jose is dynamic and ambitious.'

She argued that, together, with the support of Jacob, her son-in-law, her three sons could make it work. It was a compelling argument, I thought, and said, 'Okay, let us discuss the proposal.' She was then joined by her elder son Alexander whom I was meeting professionally for the first time.

By taking control of the firm along with the risks involved in a highly vulnerable industry, what became evident was the faith and confidence he had in himself as well as the capabilities of his brothers. I had a sense that the remarkable dynamism and drive of young Jose was going to be an influencing factor.

There were significant differences between what the family felt they could offer to Nayar and what he expected as the minimum sum for giving up his controlling stake in Choice Canning Company. However, after several rounds of discussions, the issue was finally settled. A certain agreed amount would be paid to Nayar in instalments over some time. The deal was done. Choice Canning Company now belonged to the family of the late O.C. Thomas.

So, in 1973, Choice Canning Company was restarted under the leadership of O.T. Alexander, with Tom and Jose as partners. Over the ensuing months, Choice started flourishing, thanks to Alexander's efforts. Export deals were struck with American and Japanese companies and the volumes grew substantially.

By 1975, the company had surplus funds in the shape of deposits in many banks. That phase ended a year later as the family faced another turmoil leading to Alexander's exit and putting the twenty-one-year-old Jose at the helm.

4

MADRAS DAYS

THE STORY OF JOSE TAKING CONTROL OF CHOICE IS ALSO the story of his eventful days in Madras, a ready sanctuary each time he rebelled against the strict control imposed by his elder brother. Alex expected his young brother to keep away from the day-to-day activities of the company. The spirited youngster started working on ideas to break free from these shackles. That is how Jose's Madras days began.

'After Choice came under our family's fold, Alex took total control. He did a good job, but wanted me to return to college, stay out of his way. He reeled in Booth Fisheries, US, one of the biggest players then to sign up as our customer and started earning tonnes of money for us. The man who facilitated this deal was Dilip Vyas, their main agent in India,' Jose recalls.

'Vyas became too close to Alex, was always visiting our house, even interfering in our family matters. This was on top of the influence Alex's wife was bringing to bear on our relationship. It did not affect my brother Tom as it did me. But Chandichen (what Alex was commonly addressed as) was almost fifteen years my senior. I decided to get away,' remembers Jose.

Jose convinced Alex that the sea-caught shrimp from the Tamil Nadu coast was worth pursuing over and above the backwater shrimp that was the main product for Booth Fisheries. He found a place to stay in central Madras before setting out on a whirlwind tour to scour the local markets from where sea shrimp came to Madras—the southern-most coastlines of India, Mandapam, Pamban, also Thiruchendur, a fishing hamlet once under Dutch occupation.

'The image of me idling away time on the stone benches at the Mandapam railway station, waiting for the next consignment of shrimp to arrive in the parcel bogie of the local train is still deeply etched in my mind,' says Jose, travelling back in time. Pretty soon, Jose was able to procure white shrimp that the Japanese buyers were keen to buy.

'That was the time Mitsubishi started a full-fledged office in Kochi, giving a huge boost to the exporting community of Kerala. The reason was the warmth with which Mitsubishi head of operations, Saka Moto, took to the local exporters. He would go all out to see that the Kerala exporters made a good earning. The list of those who made a pile of cash, thanks to Mitsubishi, was a long one. Choice was one of them,' says Jose.

'I decided I had to seize this opportunity so I went to Saka Moto, told him that I was ready to supply him a steady line of sea-caught shrimp from Mandapam. I never expected all the big sharks to rush to Mandapam. Suddenly, I was caught short as there was no way I could match their volumes. As the big fish from back home turned Mandapam into a new battlefield, I was muscled out. I lost a pile of money for Choice. Alex was furious and ordered me to pack my bags. Once back in

Kochi, I was banned from all company activities. It was like I was no longer a part of Choice,' he recalls.

That forced period of inactivity made Jose even more restless and rebellious. For the first time, he began toying with idea of starting his own company, thus getting himself out of Alex's control. Over the next couple of weeks, he decided to set off to Madras for a second innings. After much convincing, his mother came around and so did Alex. Jose began the journey in his old family car, accompanied by a trusted driver.

He remembers that trip particularly well also because of a small incident. They had stopped at a roadside lodge for the night in an isolated town called Kallakurichi, a seemingly ordinary town after Coimbatore on the old Madras highway. As soon as he hit the bed in his room, Jose immediately fell asleep.

He woke up next morning to a lot of noise from outside and stepped out of the room to be greeted by the sight of a number of scantily clad women of mixed age group. They were calling out to the youngster, making lewd gestures.

'I was so scared I told my driver to start the car. As our car sped out into the main road, my driver sheepishly admitted that it was a red-light area. As we drove into Madras, I was taken up with self-doubts. If this was what a small town could do to me, then I had to be wary of what awaited me in Madras. Fortunately, I would be so engrossed in making my business a success that I would have no time to be distracted by anything else,' recalls Jose with a brooding smile.

Jose now enjoyed one advantage, of having been around earlier in Madras. He started keeping track of the arrival, often many hours late, of the trains carrying loads of frozen fish, like the Howrah Express and the Kakkinada Express. As most of the wholesale fish trade was controlled by people from the

Malabar region, he found it easy to keep track of how many cases went to whom and to which market. It helped Jose no end that Malayalam was the language of choice in that circle.

He stayed in a lodge in Poonamalee High Road. He began doing the rounds, dividing time between Virugambakkam, Chintadripet, 150-year-old wholesale shrimp market in the city, the Central Railway Station and the Wall Tax Road market. The Wall Tax Road, lying adjacent to the Chennai Central Railway Station, runs parallel to the railway tracks and boasts of history dating back to the eighteenth century.

The wall, from which the name finds its origin, was built around 1773 by the British, a couple of decades after they gained control over the city of Madras from the French in 1749. The trigger for building the wall was Hyder Ali whose invading army got dangerously close to the city in 1767. A 50-feet road was built, the cost was to be recovered from the people through a tax, which never materialized.

A shrimp market opened shop over fifty years ago at the intersection of the Wall Tax Road and the Old Jail Road. The advantage was that this market was built almost parallel to Platform No. 14 of the central station, where most of the shrimp that arrived from other towns was auctioned.

It was sheer coincidence that a company called Bombay Ammonia (Madras) Pvt Ltd that began operations in Madras only a couple of years ago in 1977 would be scouting for new clients, however small. They manufactured inorganic chemicals, basically cooling materials for industrial use, with the seafood in its main radar. While they had their office on Mount Road, Bombay Ammonia also maintained a few cold storages in the city suburbs, in Virugambakkam.

Bombay Ammonia was also engaged in the supply and erection of refrigeration plants. It had around that period ventured into renting or leasing out refrigerated space ready for the use of those engaged in the business of seafood processing, especially those who could afford to put up their own plants. This is where Jose found a foothold in a business that he knew but could not afford to set up from scratch in a city like Madras. Thus began his new business in Virugambakkam.

'There he had four seafood processing units with ready-to-use refrigeration facilities and a few tables for peeling shrimp. I rented out one such unit of 100 feet by 60 feet and began running Choice Marine Products, a new company that I floated. I brought sixteen workers, all of them young women with experience in peeling shrimp from back home,' says Jose who felt for the first time that he was getting somewhere.

The young women he brought from Kochi had absolute faith in Jose as otherwise they would not have come to Madras. There were about a dozen of them and their young boss rented out a house in the neighbourhood. Their loyalty came to the fore when Jose began running out of capital. Many of them offered him their gold bangles, earrings and some even their gold chains to be pawned on behalf of Jose with a local money lender.

'The irony was, I would use the money thus borrowed to pay their own salary. Such was their implicit faith in me, they never complained, not even when they realized the business was going downhill. Being women in a male-dominated society, it would have been natural for them to be wary of me, but they offered their complete trust and I never broke it. To them, I was their protector, who would keep them safe in a dangerous city. This I did, till the very last day.'

Around that time, his driver, Noorudeen, who also dabbled as an automobile mechanic, got him an old Willy's jeep from the Madras used-vehicle market. This would be used for his regular trips to the Wall Tax market to buy shrimp for his processing unit in Vurugambakkam.

During this time, an incident took place that left a deep impression on Jose's psyche. Once, while driving on the Wall Tax Road, a few crates of shrimp fell off his jeep. Without a moment's hesitation, Jose got down on all fours and started picking them up, piece by piece. There was angry honking as traffic got held up; idle pedestrians stopped in bewilderment to gawk at this rare sight.

'That scene is still vividly fresh in my memory as if it had happened only the other day. It was not easy for me to leave the shrimp for which I had paid good money and drive away. Business was not doing too great as I was struggling to make ends meet. The bubble was due to burst any time,' adds Jose.

But then, he had had a few more irons in the fire. Jose had begun juggling a few verticals, a strategy that he would follow throughout his career. Earlier, in 1973, before he had started Choice Marine Products, Jose had presented himself at the south Indian head office of Sumitomo Corporation, Japan, in those days known as Sumitomo Shoji Kaisha Ltd in Teynampet, the upmarket commercial hub of Madras.

Sreenivasan S., who retired as senior deputy general manager of Sumitomo Corporation in 2003, recalls the day when he was a junior officer and arranged a meeting for the managing director of Choice, Kochi, with the head of Sumitomo South India operations, Shida San.

Sreenivasan says, 'The office boy brought me a note saying the managing director of the Kochi firm Choice Canning had arrived. To my surprise, a very lean adolescent, evidently in his teens, entered the office. I was astounded when my office boy told me he was the managing director. Those were the days when Japanese firms like Sumitomo were extremely reluctant to enter into deals with youngsters as they put a premium on grey hair and wisdom that comes only with age. However, being the youngest recruit in the company myself, I decided to make a pitch for the youngster.

'After speaking to the young man, I was impressed by the way he explained his plans. There was a fire in his belly, hunger in his eyes. Despite being so young, his vision was very clear. He seemed to exude the kind of confidence that had the power to rub off on others. I then called my manager to talk about Jose. The first question from Shida San was why I wanted to entertain such a young boy.

'Somehow I convinced my boss that the youngster's proposal was worth listening to. The issue was settled when I took full responsibility for all future interactions with Jose. Their discussion was fruitful. Choice, represented by Jose, joined the select list of frozen shrimp suppliers for Sumitomo,' he adds.

Jose acknowledges he did turn up for the Sumitomo meeting as a representative of his parent company. But he was still a partner at Choice. That helped him get the Japanese company on board. Jose had many hats to wear—Choice, his own company, and pretty soon, Princess Seafood.

All that would come to pass a few months after he was banished from Madras for the second consecutive time. Perhaps if he had been satisfied with merely being the official representative of Choice, things would not have headed south that fast. But much of his energy was consumed by his new baby, Choice Marine Products. Jose's plan to divide time between his parent company and the new one often meant he had time for neither at crucial moments. Soon, he began losing money. Not only was his new company in trouble, but even the Madras operations of Choice began running up losses.

His finances were in shambles. The going got tough with each passing day. The writing was clearly on the wall. Only, it took some time for Jose to read it right. Alex was furious.

'I had messed up again. In order to cut the losses, he asked me to dump everything and return. I was back in Kochi once again, consumed by dark thoughts. I was out of favour and out of luck. I had no way of getting into the thick of things at Choice, even though I was still a partner. I felt like a failure the second time around,' says Jose with complete candour.

What followed was not unlike the convalescing period of a person who had fallen ill. Eventually, the illness passed, as did the weakness. Jose decided to return to Madras, by now his safe go-to place, for the third time. Once again, he touched base with his old associates. He rented a house in the city outskirts where he occupied the ground floor. A local couple lived on the first floor.

It was an isolated locality, a fair distance away from other houses; the saving grace was the presence of Julie, a dog he had brought along from Kochi. So here was Jose, afraid of the dark and of the spirits, staying all alone in a house, which he believed was haunted. He struggled to sleep as his father's spirit kept visiting him in his dreams.

He went on a long drive and when he reached home, it was as if he had woken up from a long nightmare. He was no longer haunted by his father's spirit.

Right from the days during his second trip to Madras, there were a few relatives he would visit, to get away from the monotony of his life, which was centred around the procurement and sale of shrimp. He continued to cultivate these contacts during his final visit as well. One of them was the famous Manjila's family, a name synonymous with Malayalam cinema at one point of time.

'Frankly, I always wanted to meet the legendary actor who would later turn director—Kamal Haasan. So I used to frequent the San Thome house of M.O. Joseph, one of the biggest producers of Malayalam films, whose wife, Kunjamma, was related to the Olassayil family. It was their children who started calling me Chemmeen Jose and that name stuck for a few years. There were quite a few Malayali families who kept me going in Madras, like George Vattakunnel and Aniyamma. Between these families, some trusted colleagues and associates, I began treating Madras as my second home,' Jose reminisces.

Jose had started seeking avenues to export the shrimp processed at the Virugambakkam plant leased out by Bombay Ammonia. The likelihood was that he would have turned to some middleman to find a suitable export avenue, but that is not what fate held in store for him.

The turning point came when he caught the attention of Dhurvendra Prakash Goel (popularly called DP), among the most influential shipping agents in Madras in those days and the scion of Sri Prakash Goel, the owner of New India Shipping Agencies Pvt Ltd.

They were one of the more established steamer agents in India providing cargo services to various destinations across the globe. As they were also into handling refrigerated cargo, they came to hear of a new kid on the block called Jose carrying out a small operation in Virukkambakkam.

'One day, I was in the Virugambakkam processing plant when I heard a roaring sound and soon a red Ford Mustang revved up in front of our unit. A man sporting sunglasses stepped out and I thought it was a Bollywood star! It was

DP and he had come to discuss terms and conditions about sourcing cargo from me,' says Jose.

Over the weeks that followed, Jose began bonding with DP, taken up as much by his glamour as his affluent lifestyle. At that point of time, Jose's biggest ambition undoubtedly was to groom himself after DP. He was thrilled when his new friend invited him to board a ship. It sparked a chord in him as it was a dream from his Mattancherry days finally coming true.

DP introduced Jose to his father, Sri Prakash (SP), who was a giant in the shipping business. The latter took an immediate liking to Jose and started addressing him as 'my son'. Perhaps Jose reminded him of his younger days when he too was new in business with no one to support him.

'Then he invited me home for dinner and I was mesmerized by the sheer opulence of what I could only think of as a mansion! The gleaming imported marble on the floor reflected my face. The dining room was massive, the table large enough to seat a few dozen. There was an army of helpers waiting on us. For the first time, I got to see at close quarters how the truly rich lived. And I began wondering why I too could not lead such a life,' recalls Jose with a wistful smile.

Then one day, SP asked Jose about the seafood business during a casual interaction. He replied it was a good business provided there was sufficient capital. He opened up to the old man that his business was run on borrowed capital.

'I told him how this could be transformed into a big business if sufficient funds could be found. SP patted me on my back and said he would provide the funds. That is how Princess Seafood was born. Thus, I became the managing director of a company. I was all of twenty-one years old,' adds Jose.

This was the chance of a lifetime; Jose seized it with both hands. He started pushing Princess Seafood with vigour. Despite the financial backing of SP, Jose began to borrow heavily from banks as that was the only way he could sustain the scaled-up volumes. This period also saw Jose pushing hard to gain a toehold in the shipping sector. He started interacting with the elite of Madras—some of whom were big-time shipping agents.

His Madras dreams came crashing down for the third time as DP's shipping activities faced a meltdown. The spin-off effect was most telling on Princess Seafood which had major exposure to DP's New India Maritime Agency. It was during the days of Emergency declared by Indira Gandhi that DP's father, Sri Prakash, was arrested, citing violation of COFEPOSA (Conservation of Foreign Exchange and Prevention of Smuggling Act) that dealt a shattering blow to Jose's life, too.

Smelling trouble, banks began cracking down on all enterprises that DP was associated with. Princess Seafood was no exception. Soon, Jose had lending institutions breathing down his neck. It all collapsed like a pack of cards as Princess Seafood, in its pursuit of the large volume model, was hugely leveraged.

With DP all but disappearing from the equation, Jose was left holding a huge volume of shrimp that was in the hold for export from Princess Seafood. He tried to liquidate it by going to Sumitomo, but with the rider that they had to buy the consignment only if they were satisfied with the quality check.

Sreenivasan recalls, 'Our team went for an inspection to his rented factory premises on Gollavar Agraharam Road in Tondiarpet. Princess Seafood had a workforce of around eighty people. It was during that time that the most defining moment of his life happened. We were inspecting the block-frozen prawn slabs in his factory's central hall where the melting blocks were lined up. Suddenly, we realized that one of the old shrimp blocks had been replaced by a fresh block by one of Jose's supervisors.'

Srinivasan still remembers the shrill voice of Shida San shouting that the Japanese were ready to accept mistakes but would not tolerate cheating or being untruthful. Things started looking pretty bleak as Shida San insisted that he would settle for nothing short of blacklisting Jose's company by Sumitomo. For Jose, it was like his worst nightmare had come true.

Jose was literally in tears as he kept repeating that he was not involved, that his supervisor had acted on his own. To his dismay, it was clear that the Japanese national did not believe him. The damage was done. And a big lesson learnt the hard way.

Jose came to the conclusion that losing honour was worse than death itself. Despair took over, the young man started thinking of taking the honourable way out. Was the impending loss so catastrophic that the youngster would be forced to contemplate ending his life? Or was there more to the story? Jose still shudders when he tries to recall those momentous hours that had the potential to either make or break his life.

'To put it plainly, the Japanese thought I had cheated. I remember what happened quite clearly. The sample taken from the consignment from the held-over Princess Seafood that was to be exported was on one side of the hall, ready for inspection. On the other side was fresh shrimp, the two sides divided by a chest-high partition, a kind of half wall. The Japanese team, including their Madras head, Shida San, was in an adjoining room along with me,' confides Jose, wracked by memories of one of the lowest points of his life.

'I was told later by my staff that at that juncture our supervisor, Devassikutty, vaulted over the half wall and swapped the old shrimp with the fresh lot. I saw Shida San suddenly rush into the hall where he caught Devassikutty red-handed. What followed was a terrible dream. Shida San started shouting at the top of his voice and I feared all of it was directed at me. I was overcome by shame,' he says, virtually reliving arguably one of the darkest hours of his life.

'Since it was my employee who had committed the fraud, I had to take full responsibility. It was such a severe loss of face that I wanted to end my life that night. It was Cheenu (Sreenivasan) who stopped me and then drafted a letter to the Sumitomo management, owning up to the grave mistake. In the letter, there was also an impassioned appeal to allow me to correct the mistake,' recalls Jose, drawing a deep breath.

'Later, it was again Cheenu who appealed to his superiors to take a lenient view, to give me a second chance. I had lost face. As per the Japanese code of conduct, and in mine too, death was a better option than one filled with shame,' he adds.

Sreenivasan points out, 'Later that night, I met Jose in his hotel room. He was in a dangerous mood, threatening to jump from his third-floor balcony. He kept saying he wanted to end his life. He was totally shattered by the shame it caused him. It took all my skills to console him.'

The stage was set for the final withdrawal of Jose from Madras. There were huge debts to be settled with banks. The Olassayil family pulled the hapless Jose out of Madras.

His mother and his eldest brother-in-law came down to help him relocate.

'As I had managed to pick up some good pieces of furniture, Ammachy, my mother, had clear plans as to which items would go where in our Kochi house. She probably felt that those would be permanent reminders about the little things salvaged from my disastrous Madras adventure. I could not give her even that satisfaction. Bhadran Mattel, the aspiring film director whom I knew from old days in Pala, met me and asked why I wanted to take the trouble of lugging old furniture back to my ancestral house,' recalls Jose.

'Bhadran told me a famous Malayalam film actress, wished to check out my old furniture. He said she would drop in and pay by cheque if she found everything to her liking. Apparently, she did like it because she took it all away. It did not agree with my mother's conservative outlook that I was giving away my household items to an actress. She was furious as she said I was in no position to be handing out favours. As I recall, the cheque bounced, vindicating my mother's standpoint,' says Jose, brushing off the suggestion that he may have been smitten by the actress.

Revisiting the snapshots of Jose's Madras experience, there were quite a few positive takeaways too. There was this journey of twenty-two-year-old Jose, accompanied by his brother, Tom, twenty-three, going on their first overseas journey—to Far East Asia, mainly Japan, intending to meet one of the heads of Sumitomo Corporation, Nishiama San. They were to proceed to Europe, and the US in 1976, making it more of a world tour.

The journey got off to a dramatic start at the Calcutta Airport when the young man faced his first test of character.

Those days, the foreign exchange allowed per person was $500. A well-meaning uncle had persuaded him to take an additional $500 which was hidden away in his suitcase.

Now, picture this—the two brothers, both in their early twenties. Short, dark-skinned, long-haired, clad in high-waist bellbottoms, broad belts with flashy buckles and dark aviators.

The customs officers are trained to single out those who breach the law as much from their general appearance as their body language. They asked Jose whether he was carrying unapproved currency. His vehement denial only reinforced their suspicions. They decided to check his bags.

As the officers began rummaging through his luggage, Jose started praying for a reprieve. It was then that he made the promise that he would never do anything untruthful again. To his horror, he saw his father's Omega wristwatch fall down and the glass case shatter.

The watch was not his but was bequeathed to his brother Alex, following their father's passing. Among three prized possessions, a gold ring, a gold chain and the Omega watch, all of which was always seen on O.C. Thomas when he was alive. Alex had got the watch, Tom the ring, and Jose, being the youngest son, the chain. Alex had asked him to get the watch repaired at the authorized Omega outlet in New York.

It was not just an expensive watch; it had the sentimental value of a family heirloom and that watch now lying shattered on the floor of the Calcutta Airport. Naturally, in his panic, Jose was joined in by Tom as they started shouting accusatorily at the carelessness of the authorities. With placatory gestures from that of the officer, the search of the bag was abandoned abruptly. The shattered glass had provided him a lucky escape.

Jose believes that incident was a warning—a timely reminder against what could happen if he continued breaking the law or veering away the path of truth. That day he made a promise to himself that he would never indulge in unethical practices or bend the rules while doing business. It proved to be a costly promise. To this day, he believes it was this decision that kept him from climbing the heights of corporate success that some of his peers managed.

'I went on that trip not to pursue seafood business, but it was to replicate what DP was doing. It was to follow-up on a business lead that Sumitomo Corporation, with whom I had forged a close relationship those days, had given me. They had arranged a meeting with a Japanese shipping line and in my mind I had decided this would be my ticket to enter the shipping line, my aspiration then being DP and the kind of life he led in Madras,' explains Jose.

His meeting with the brass of the Japanese shipping line did not go as per script, which as Jose envisaged had only one outcome, one of triumph. When the meeting began, he was quite confident of clinching the deal. The truth is, he was not only underprepared but also overconfident—a dangerous combination.

The meeting began coming unstuck for Jose when the discussion veered around to the technical aspects of the Cochin Port, its infrastructure and its labour force. He started giving glib answers, convinced he could bluff them. That was not to be as a basic question on the draft permissibility of the Cochin harbour and the necessity to dredge the channel for bigger vessels completely floored him. The reality was, he had gone into the meeting convinced that he could win them over citing his ability to procure cargo.

'That is not how it panned out. I had erred in presuming that I could bluff my way into getting signed up as their agent in south India. That was a humiliating experience for me and I thought all my efforts to associate with the Japanese were jinxed. Perhaps that is the reason why I have always valued any kind of relationship with the Japanese. I also started travelling fairly regularly to Tokyo,' reiterates Jose.

If Japan continued to lure him, so did Madras, the city where he cut his teeth as an independent businessman. In 2020, when he decided that the Choice Group was ready for a pan-India image, it was his old port of call, Madras or Chennai, that he chose, buying a sprawling office of about 7,000 square feet in what was once the iconic Devi Theatre, owned by acclaimed Tamil actor, Sivaji Ganesan. Fully convinced that Chennai, and not Kochi, would be his India headquarters, Jose has gone in for the outright purchase of an even larger office space in the same building.

The office premise was not chosen randomly. Many of those places which he haunted, often in sheer desperation, during three back-to-back sojourns in the mid-1970s are all located in the near vicinity, a constant reminder of the desperate paths he travelled to get where he was now.

'I came of age in Madras, going through many unforgettable experiences, getting entangled in a few misadventures. Some of them came at significant financial cost to the family. But there must have been a compelling reason for me to flee Kochi, trying to find redemption in Madras, in three back-to-back trips when I was barely out of my teens,' he rationalizes.

Jose continued to believe that there was no way any profitable activity could be taken forward without taking calculated risks. Some would pay off, others would not.

By the time he left Madras for the third time, he had come to be known as Chemmeen Jose. From that point, his life has revolved around two things—shrimp exports and shipping.

This state of affairs would continue for many years, till he would see wisdom in the first big diversion in the late 1980s. Yet, before all that were to pan out, he was to undergo a major transition of personality—from Chemmeen Jose to a suave international trader, complete with a spanking new identity.

5

RETURN OF THE PRODIGAL

THE TREMORS THAT CAUSED A MILD DISTURBANCE WITHIN the Olassayil household in the days immediately following the death of O.C. Thomas, had assumed the shape of a major quake by 1976. Curiously, it was the prodigal son who had returned defeated from Madras—that too multiple times—who emerged victorious in the battle for the family crest, Choice.

In retrospect, it could be said that the stage was set for a parting of ways. Jose was convinced he was the true heir to his father's legacy. The reasoning went along the following lines—he may not be capable of taking measured decisions like his elder brother but his passion for Choice was unmatched.

'It was clear to me that Alex wanted to get a move on. It may have been the outcome of many advising him. They may have told him that he need not carry the baggage that was the family, especially the responsibility of finding suitable alliances for and marrying off three more sisters. It made a whole lot of sense for him to get his share and strike out on his own. That is what he did,' says Jose.

'As my father had died intestate (without leaving a will), it was the 1976 partition that decided who would get what. Alex got a pile of cash, our house in Koovapadam near Mattancherry. He could start off with a clean slate. My brother Tom and I got all the liabilities. The mediator, father's friend, Venugopal C. Govind, kept asking me if I fully realized what I was signing, probably because of my tender age. Sure, I got control of Choice, but also a mountain of debt with it. I was left holding the baggage,' Jose shed light on how he got control of the parent company.

From Alex's perspective, there was no point in triggering his young brother into fresh acts of rebellion, more often than not resulting in considerable financial loss to the undivided family assets. Add to this the fact that their mother could find little fault with her youngest son and it was an easy decision to make.

'I remember the days following our father's unexpected passing. We were all so young. I was not even thirty years old, Jose twenty and Tom just a year older. We had no option but to buy out Madhavan Nayar's stake in Choice Canning. It was then that Jose started making trips to Madras to buy raw material. He decided he wanted to do things his way and set up two independent companies, Choice Marine Products and Princess Seafood, the second with his friend DP as a silent partner. Even then, Jose was very adventurous and wanted to try out new things. Unfortunately, both ventures failed; we had to settle the debts he ran up in Madras,' says Alex.

'We somehow persuaded Jose to return home. Pretty soon, Jose made it clear that he did not wish to have me as a partner as his style of functioning was vastly different from mine. While I appreciated his frankness, I was really sad at the prospect of leaving Choice. But the decision was made and I reluctantly surrendered my share in Choice Canning. It took me another year to start National Seafood in 1978,' he adds.

'In retrospect, I feel our parting of ways was the best thing that happened for both of us. We have very different temperaments. Jose has no fear and he is not averse to risk-taking. I was more the slow and steady type. I don't think many would have picked themselves up and moved forward after facing the kind of debacles that Jose had to face, of which many around him would not get to know till he got through that phase. Jose has always run a one-man show which also is his success formula,' sums up Alex.

The details of the actual partition are explained by the man who drafted the document, Govind, who says the partition formula for Choice Canning was based on an overall agreed valuation of the net worth, assets and liabilities of the firm.

'It was agreed that running the firm with all its assets including goodwill and trade name Choice, liabilities, contingencies, staff, was to be taken over by Jose. Alex was to exit the firm by receiving a certain total agreed sum in full settlement. The entire reconstruction exercise was carried out smoothly. By late 1976, Choice Canning's board of directors had to be reconstituted, minus one. The new board had three directors: Jose, Tom and their mother Annamma,' says Govind.

'I was not part of the second restructuring of the company in 1986, when Tom opted to move out of Choice. Just as Alexander parted ways without any acrimony in 1976, a decade later Tom too dissociated from the parent company. He too could make a smooth exit as Jose offered his brother a magnanimous deal, by letting go of some of the prized family assets. Finally, Jose was the lone man holding up the banner of Choice that the patriarch O.C. Thomas considered most precious.'

By early 1977, Choice Canning was almost shut down as its principal creditor, Andhra Bank, froze the company's accounts. This was also the transition period, when the earlier board had been rendered null and void, even as a new board was yet to assume office. There was also the issue of fund shortage, with liabilities outweighing the company's net worth. In that hour of darkness came light at the end of the tunnel. Bank of India decided to extend an overdraft of ₹5 lakh.

'But our woes were far from over. Alex had walked off with the assets including a valuable property in Koovappadam and a significant amount of cash, not to mention—most of our valuable clients, including Booth Fisheries—which to be fair, Alex had handled. Tom and I were faced with the debts I had run up in Madras. So, I had to find a solution,' recounts Jose.

His mother agreed with her son's decision to sell the last large property that they owned, all of 15 acres in Edakochi. The immediate need was to repay the outstanding debt of Choice Canning which stood at ₹6 lakh.

Jose says, with a visible tinge of sadness: 'I know this—to sell one's hard-earned property, acquired by the earlier generation is as painful as the amputation of one's limb. In those days, it was also a matter of shame as it signalled desperation, always seen as a move triggered by shortage of money in the family. This was perhaps the only time that I was involved in the loss of a family asset. Because, in the following years, I have only acquired assets, be it land, building or even a factory.'

In the days and weeks that followed, Jose would turn up every day with unfailing and often irritating regularity at the Cochin Diocese Bishop's house, to meet Rt Rev Joseph Kureethra. Such visits would invariably be followed by stopping at St Joseph's Bethlehem Church, Chullickal, to meet Fr Mathew who was the priest assigned with the task of finding land for a new college that was under the active consideration of the Church.

Jose was on tenterhooks. Surely, he could not forfeit his legacy only a few months after claiming it as his birthright. He knew there would be no other buyer for such a big property in Kochi those days. He knew he was at the mercy of the Church and the priests in charge could either make or break his life. The flip side was, the priests knew they had him in a vice-like grip.

'I was caught like a deer in headlights. There was nowhere else to go. I vividly remember spending painfully long hours waiting for Fr Mathew to come out of his prayers and endless committee meetings. The only occasions he found time to say a few words, he talked about how the college project was not happening as there was no clearance from the top—the obvious reason being shortage of funds,' remembers Jose.

Each day, with this kind of feedback, his hopes began receding. He was literally losing his mind, faced with the unacceptable outcome of no sale. Little did he realize that the priests were excellent negotiators and all that negative feedback was but a ploy to beat the price down!

'Finally, Fr Mathew came up with an offer of just over ₹53,000 per acre. In short, the massive tract of land where the St Aquinas College, Edakochi, began functioning in 1981, went out from the Olassayil family fold for a mere ₹8,00,000. The sale soon happened, ownership changed hands. A bulk of that amount went towards settling our outstanding debt of ₹6,00,000 with Andhra Bank,' says Jose, winding up his narration with a sigh of relief.

With the balance amount, they started a new account with Bank of India, which essentially was the working capital for Choice Canning under Jose's stewardship. Tom remained his fierce protector and partner for the next 10 years before he too decided to part ways in 1986.

Jose would soon get used to getting pushed into tight corners. There would be no more family assets to sell but he would master the art of buying assets with money that he was yet to raise. Banks would back him to the hilt. Debtors would agree to not insist on immediate repayment. He would dream big and sell big dreams. He would also stumble many times, narrowly escaping a major fall on more than one occasion.

His journey had just begun.

6

CLOSE ENCOUNTER WITH THE JAPANESE

THE MEMORIES COME RUSHING IN SHORT BURSTS, AS IF propelled by an adrenaline rush—right from his boyhood days in Kochi to the period where he makes a mark as a wannabe tycoon in what was then called Madras. This was also a phase when he stepped on a few toes in the family in a bid to try and carve out a standalone space for himself.

Since Jose hailed from Kochi and was familiar with the coastline around it, Quilon or Kollam as that southern Kerala coastal city is now called, should have hardly figured in this narrative. Usually, Jose went for bulk purchase of chemmeen or shrimp down the coast to Alappuzha, but rarely to Quilon.

Any other year, he would have found the answer to the one big problem that he was to soon face in Purakkad beach, off the Alappuzha coast. That has always been a place renowned for the monsoon-triggered phenomenon peculiar to Kerala locally called chaakara, which translates into the aggregation of fish in the warm mud banks adjoining the sea-mouth of the backwaters. This time round, chaakara hit the Quilon beach which was where Jose got the ammunition to take on the might of a powerful Japanese trading conglomerate.

Jose fondly and often recalls that his entire life's journey has been about getting his father's approval—an obsession that he evidently refused to give up even after his father's death. That is how he rationalizes his—what others consider impetuous or reckless—actions. While most of these spurts of frenzied activities were risky, there was only one occasion when he played dirty—to get even with yet another Japanese company.

During the late 1970s, Jose could often be found at the Mandapam railway station late into the night, waiting for the next batch of shrimp from the fishers who ploughed the sea between India and Sri Lanka. He was still in his early twenties when he cast aside caution by taking on a well-renowned Japanese trading corporation, for failure to keep their promise. The battle cry from Jose was, no matter how big the company, it has to pay the price when it reneges on a deal.

Let's take a quick look back to 1976. Young Jose had grabbed the opportunity to spearhead Choice activities in Madras. Naturally, he was out to prove his mettle, both to his elder brother who had just taken over the reins of the company from his late father, and also his mother. After his father's premature demise, it was his mother who occupied the pedestal as the head of the family. Those were the days when the Japanese companies played middlemen and imported shrimp from India. This would be re-exported to the US after value-addition, but on scaled up margins.

'I wished to handle our Japanese clients. However, Alex, who was the boss, said no. Unlike me, he was averse to risk-taking and quite careful in his dealings. The India operation of the Japanese company was based out of Mumbai, then Bombay. I was to meet the India head, Mr Alvares, who hailed from Goa,' Jose recalls.

'Soon it became apparent from the words exchanged between Alvares and the two Japanese nationals working with him, that they considered me an *otokonoko*—a little boy,' says Jose. 'I somehow convinced them of my credentials and clinched a contract to deliver 20,000 cases of 71–91 size shrimp at $2 per kg. Alex was also happy with this arrangement since it was a competitive price. I returned to Kochi and began scouting the beaches to secure bulk orders,' he continues the narration.

'Lady luck finally smiled on me, something that had been eluding me for long. The news started trickling in that the chakara had hit Quilon beach where shrimp had accumulated in large quantities. I rushed to Quilon where I started getting it at throwaway rates, such was the availability. The shrimp had to be removed from the beach on a war footing, which is what I did.'

'The Japanese company with which I had signed a contract began getting offers at half my rate. That is when Alvares opened my letter of credit (LC) which was only for a limited tenure. At the same time, the vessel that was set to pick up the cargo received a message to cancel the trip. Soon, the LC expired and I was left high and dry with 20,000 cases of worthless shrimp. Alvares refused to relent despite it being clear that the ship cancelling its trip was not my fault,' he adds.

Soon, Alvares agreed to renew the contract at new terms, the new rate fixed at 50 cents per kilo. Jose was caught in a bind. He knew something was wrong as the Japanese company officials refused to meet him. Without discussing it with Alex, he agreed to the new terms, in an attempt to minimize the loss. Alex was furious.

'That is when I started scouring Kollam beaches for the remains of the chakara and found truckloads of shrimp that had started turning bad. I shipped the company their consignment which included large quantities of rotten shrimp from the Quilon beach. I got paid as per the new rates, a quarter of what I was originally promised. I felt it was only fair that they got what they paid for,' says Jose.

Once the consignment landed in Japan, they found out what had happened. To pre-empt any legal action, Jose sent them a letter explaining the sequence of events that led him to take such a drastic step. He conveyed to the company bosses in Japan that he felt cheated by their Indian office, prompting him to retaliate. The management relented.

It was Jose unfettered—the raw force of a youngster who decided to fight for what he felt was an injustice that was meted out to him. For once, the rules of the game did not apply as he allowed himself to join the slugfest.

In the following years, Jose would make multiple trips to Tokyo. It took him a couple of years and a dozen trips to overcome his fear that the particular Japanese company had him marked out as enemy number one. It is quite unlikely that they would have recorded this episode anywhere in their minutes!

Jose prefers to believe there would be some note somewhere that recounts how they got wind of the malpractices in their India office, leading to a few sackings at the senior level.

It is not an incident he takes pride in. It was, perhaps, the first and the last time Jose had traded blows with a partner who turned the tables on him. Sure, he never really visited the Quilon beach again but the image of the chakara remains etched in his memory as vividly as the smell of the rotting shrimp.

7

MALDIVES MAGIC

IN 1977, THE SEAFOOD FOOD INDUSTRY WAS FLOURISHING in Kochi. Exporting cargo and converting goods to cash was a sort of liberation. Then there were the magical names in the shipping industry—Oceanic Seafoods, Esmario Marine, C. Cherian, Poopally Brothers, the Anthrapers, India Seafood, Southern Seafood and Edward & Sons Trading Co—who straddled the scene like virtual giants.

The Choice Group was barely a drop in the ocean, especially as it was still reeling from the internal bifurcation that meant many of their clients had shifted loyalties to National Seafood, the company floated by Alex.

The new management, with young Jose at its helm, was forced to down the shutters of the company for the next few months as the bankers froze its accounts. Finally, it was the Andhra Bank that came up with a bailout plan—a loan amount of ₹5 lakh.

Meanwhile, the Israel–Egypt war began in 1976 leading to the closure of Suez Canal throwing international cargo movement into total disarray. The repercussions were felt right across the globe. Cochin port was no exception; surplus cargo started piling up. There was complete desolation in the air as no ships came calling.

Then came the breakthrough. Shipping lines started with a new international route, completely bypassing the Suez Canal. News broke that ships were on their way to Cochin to pick up cargo. Those ships would then head out to the US East Coast via the Cape of Good Hope.

Jose recalls, 'The entire exporting community was in the doldrums. It was at this time of distress that Tuticorin-based Nadar & Co advertised in the weekly *Shipping Times* that they were planning to bring a Norwegian vessel to Kochi via the Cape of Good Hope. Interested participants had to collect the prospectus via telex. To me, it felt like an opportunity to enter shipping was beckoning me. I simply had to heed that calling, as I had done in the past when opportunities opened up first in the form of Gillette blades and then, betel nuts.'

When the news broke, it created a buzz in the shipping community. Jose had two reasons to be excited—he was desperate to export his goods and he also was especially keen to see the vessel that soon docked at Berth 3 at Cochin port's Ernakulam Wharf. The crew stayed at Hotel Sealord. According to Jose, Nadar must have made more than ₹3 crore with that transaction, such were the margins those days.

Jose decided to meet Nadar's son and introduce himself. He also set up a meeting with Capt. Gopalan, the shore captain who was the one that had persuaded the company to make him an agent to solicit cargo. Capt. Gopalan asked him to come to Chennai. The task was cut out for him—he had to convince Capt. Menon of Maldives Shipping, who along with his colleagues Capt. Gopalan and Capt. Ricky, would turn mentors to Jose in his journey as a shipping agent, that he was confident about soliciting the required volume of cargo. Jose succeeded! His shipping dreams were about to come true.

'I could not believe that I was going to be introduced to Maldives Shipping—the national line of the Maldives government. Capt. Menon was already doing business with Maldives Shipping by placing their vessels mostly in Madras. After this meeting, I was told that if Choice Shipping (then called TeeJay Shipping) could find cargo from Cochin to the Red Sea area—mainly Djibouti, Sudan and Jeddah—a vessel could be arranged to call at Cochin. But they wanted guaranteed projection of how much cargo I could arrange, and in how many days I could dispatch the vessel from Cochin port,' says Jose, travelling down memory lane.

Once back in Cochin, Jose received a telex message: 'A vessel is going to become available in Karachi. It could reach Kochi. Cargo is needed. Please provide the prospects.' Those days Mattancherry was the hub of spice and tea trade, with the bulk of traders belonging to the Gujarati community. Tea was exported to Sudan, Egypt; spices to Yemen, Sudan.

The excitement grew in Jose and he just could not believe that a vessel was going to call under his agency at Cochin. Now, he had to find the cargo. His old connections at the Mattancherry market came to his rescue as he rushed to meet with Shafi, his betel nut business associate from many years ago.

'I knew he would be able to help me. He then introduced me to another Gujarati merchant who was one of the major exporters of Indian spices to the Red Sea ports. It was that merchant who introduced me to various other tea exporters who used to trade in the Red Sea area,' says Jose.

He could not have chosen a worse time to persuade them to do business with a new shipping line as they were still reeling from a disastrous engagement about six months ago with an unknown shipping line from Asia. After accepting a full load of cargo comprising spices, tea and coffee, the ship went to the Chinese coast. Their customer sold the ship and disappeared with the cargo. Therefore, it was a tough task cut out for Jose—to solicit cargo for Maldives Shipping from the very same traders who were still smarting from their recent loss!

To make matters worse for him, Shipping Corporation of India, the Indian government-owned shipping line, had won the traders over. It was stability they were looking at, after the incident of the runaway vessel.

'This being the case, I found it very difficult to convince them. Finally, I told them that the shipping line I was representing was also government-owned, it had the full backing of the Maldives government. It took some doing, but eventually, I won them over. With their support assured, I went back to Capt. Menon to provide him with the details of cargo, its nature and volume. He made one thing clear—unless I could find 8,000 metric tonnes of cargo to fill the empty vessel, Maldives Shipping would seek out other ports with assured cargo,' he added.

Meanwhile, Shipping Corporation of India sought a letter from the President of Maldives to stand guarantee for the cargo, knowing full well that that was certainly not going to happen. It looked as if Jose's maiden entry into the world of shipping would be short-lived.

Yet, things worked out as they often do in the last minute and *Maldives Republic* was cleared for docking at the Cochin port.

The vessel was allowed to berth only after thirty-five days but Jose did not let on this little fact to the shipping company in Bombay. He tried every trick in the book including 'sick person on board' to cut through the waiting period. But there was trouble brewing elsewhere.

To his dismay, Jose could manage to arrange only 5,000 metric tonnes, almost 40 per cent short of the target volume. Though they promised to make up the next time, he had not factored in the inability of the exporters to deliver at short notice. Some of these exporters, like Vikram Dholakhia, Ashwin Shah and Naveen Shah, subsequently became Jose's friends but that was for another day. Right then, he had to solve the immediate problem.

He had to take a call—either give up or commit to deliver 8,000 metric tonnes, complicit in the knowledge that he would be falling woefully short. He decided to take the bold step, and confirmed a full cargo. Based on this, Maldives Shipping confirmed that *Maldives Republic* would be arriving in Cochin port with a maximum turnaround time of 72 hours. Jose went all out and made all arrangements with port and customs authorities, hired employees who had experience in handling vessels and port formalities. The excitement grew and sleepless nights followed as there were ten days to go before the vessel would reach Cochin. It was the hour of reckoning for the young boy who gazed across the sea from the shores of his hometown and dreamt of mastering the seas.

Jose made fervent appeals to the merchants to augment their volume, so that he could get closer to the 8,000-tonne target. As *Maldives Republic* docked in the harbour, Jose told himself that he was finally a steamer agent like DP. He dreamt about the Ford Mustang and the palatial mansions he too would build. The vessel berthed, and if he was being honest, it was the first time Jose was seeing a cargo ship at such close quarters! The manner in which he had pitched himself to Capt. Menon, he was never asked about his experience in ship handling. Had he been asked, he would have had to say that he had none, or would have had to lie, which he had promised himself never to do after the Calcutta airport mishap.

'Fortunately for me, Capt. Menon assumed I knew shipping. It was my good fortune to have hired the right employees like Vijayan. Hence, everything took place smoothly, including berthing the vessel to repairs and refueling, which by itself was an eye-opener for Jose.

Then the real issues started cropping up, one after the other. It was confirmed that the cargo availability would not be more than 5,000 tonnes. Normally, the loading was carried out by the stevedores and their head was known to Jose. He started planning his way out of the mess as he feared they would fire him and also claim damages. He hardly had the financial capability to handle the vessel leave alone pay any claims and damages.

'I reached out to the head of stevedores and sought his help, opening up to him about the ground reality. He asked me what I had in mind. I asked him to go slow with the loading. I remember that man laughing his head off, exclaiming, "Dear son, you don't know the basics of shipping."'

Jose's office received a telex message that the Marine Superintendent of Maldives Shipping, Captain Ricky, was reaching Cochin to oversee ship repairs and certifications. As Jose went to receive him at the old Cochin airport, he knew once they got through the formalities, the captain would ask to turn to the business at hand.

Jose waited at the airport, tension mounting by the minute, as a small propeller-driven aircraft landed and a 6 feet 3 inches-tall and fair-skinned gentleman stepped down the ladder. Capt. Ricky got into Jose's car, lit his pipe, asked him a few questions in his husky voice, making full eye contact.

'I was literally shivering as I was forced to lie while I drove him to the Malabar Hotel where he asked me to wait in the lobby. Then I drove him to port to board *Maldives Republic*. Capt. Ricky was so experienced I was sure he would soon catch on. As he walked up ship's gangway, my inexperience must have been writ large even in the way I struggled to follow him,' remembers Jose. 'After finding his way to the deck and walking around for a while, Ricky took me to the captain's cabin and asked, "What have you done? Where is the promised cargo?" I was at a loss for words but somehow blurted out, "Sir. I am sorry." He roared back at me that I could not say sorry and escape the consequences as my incompetence was going to not only cause high financial damages but also affect the credibility of a shipping line,' he recalled with a grimace.

Jose still cannot erase the image of Captain Ricky glaring at him, with smoke spewing out of his pipe as it would out of a steam engine. Ricky's fury had to be seen to be believed when he questioned Jose about his experience in the field of shipping and Jose mumbled it was his maiden venture.

Ricky's face held an incredulous look as he spoke in a menacing tone, 'You had the audacity to get a vessel that costs millions of dollars to call under your agency? Your game is over. Captain, there is no more cargo, close the hatch and sail to the Red Sea.'

After the vessel had sailed, Ricky called Jose to his hotel room. Then they began to speak openly. 'I confessed that I did not know anything about shipping. Then I started narrating my life story—my desire to get into shipping, my contacts with the exporters, and so on. I pleaded for another chance so that I could prove to Maldives Shipping what I was capable of. He smiled and said, "I will admit one thing, you have guts", Jose opens up about how he really entered shipping.

Jose then came to know that Ricky had called the Maldives operation hub and told them that due to technical reasons, the vessels could not be fully loaded. By covering up for Jose and protecting him from instant sacking, Ricky had made a life-long friend. 'Years later, Ricky told me that he knew instantly from the vague answers I had given him and the unsure way in which I had walked up the gangway of *Maldives Republic* that I was a novice to shipping,' says Jose with a rueful smile.

'Ricky began training me in the intricacies of shipping including marine insurance, claims, disputes and so on. It took us only about three years to enter into a relationship where Ricky treated me as his son. He was based in Bombay, the India HQ of Maldives Shipping, where I would be a regular guest at his residence,' he adds.

Within a few months, Jose succeeded in cementing his relationship with the Maldives Shipping senior management, mostly based out of Bombay and some in Madras. His chief pointsman those days was Ahmed Mujtaba, the South East Asia Head of Maldives Shipping, with his base in Bombay.

Mujtaba would later go on to join the Cabinet during the presidency of Maumoon Abdul Qayyoom as Minister of Transport & Shipping, and then the chief coordinator to execute political reforms in the country by President Mohammed Waheed Hassan Manik and president of Human Rights Commission of Maldives.

'I remember it was Mujtaba who always had his eye on me—he kept throwing opportunities in my direction, all the while keenly monitoring if I was slipping up. Sure, it was preferential treatment when seen from my eyes but for him, apparently having the Maldivian vessels loaded in Kochi meant a lesser turnaround time than the busy ports of Karachi and Bombay, and way lesser parking fee, with each vessel saving around $80,000, which I was not aware of. I will never forget that he kept pushing me to procure more assured cargo,' Jose recalls.

In the next couple of years, hundreds of Maldives vessels would call at Cochin port under Jose's agency, thus setting him on course to fulfilling his fervent dream—to become another DP.

Jose had always believed in going after windfall opportunities. While some of them have famously backfired, there have been many instances where his quick responses when opportunities came knocking, have earned him serious money.

Hence, he had no reason to lose time weighing the pros and cons when Aswin Shah, representing tea exporting house Madhu Jayanti, belonging to the Gujarati community in Mattancherry, tipped him off that there was big money to be made if he was willing to take some risk. He simply jumped at the opportunity.

'Aswin said a strike had broken out at the Calcutta port. He further asked if I knew that many kilo tonnes of tea was stuck there. In those days, Calcutta port handled all the tea trade from India and this opened up a huge window of opportunity. A plan was quickly formulated that I would try and get Indian Railways to have the entire cargo moved from Calcutta to Cochin using covered BCXT wagons, each with a capacity to carry 55.5 tonnes. I was onto something big,' said Jose as he relived those days of adrenalin rush.

He had Maldives Shipping vessels ready to reach Cochin and ship out the commodity to its destinations spread across the world. He also engaged with Indian Railways, booking bogies of goods trains by the dozens to bring all that tea from Calcutta to Cochin.

Jose had, in his mind, begun counting thick wads of notes, the fresh smell of new currency wafting across the air, when reality struck. The Maldivian vessels had reached Cochin port but the first train had not. Given that it cost the ship $10,000 as berthing charge each day, any delay meant the profits dwindling rapidly by that amount each passing day. When it appeared as if his pipedream would go up in smoke, Jose started doing what he now knew he does best—fire-fighting!

'It was only later that I came to know the train was held back at Shoranur Junction on account of shunting. But with no train in sight and the ship already berthed, I had no clue how to respond to the angry calls from my friends in Maldives Shipping. My immediate response—something I would continue to do when faced with stress—was to go and hide myself in a room at the Malabar Hotel, now Taj Malabar, for the next two days. Sure, I lost a bit of money but thereafter it began raining money,' says Jose.

Perhaps it did not quite rain money but money did begin to come in, in a manner he had hitherto not witnessed. For a young man starved of funds for long, especially for one who had been struggling to make ends meet with his main business in the seafood sector, it was no surprise that Jose thought it was raining money. This lasted till the strike in Calcutta port was called off a few months later.

The volume of tea Jose handled during this time resulted in a good burst of income, prompting him to open up an office in Shoranur. This was strategically located near the railway station to avoid delays in the running time of the trains due to shunting. It would also mark the onset of many more adventures for Jose. Often things worked out to his advantage, resulting in windfall gains from activities totally unconnected to his chosen field.

Those were the days when he forgot he was first and foremost an entrenched player in the seafood industry. Once he got himself positioned on the radar of Maldives Shipping, Jose began his journey as a wannabe mover and shaker in the shipping industry. While Mujtaba was his mainstay, there were two other officers who were critical to his survival as the main agent for Maldives Shipping in India.

One was Ahmed Ali Maniku who too went on to become an important player in the Maldives government. The other was Balan Nair, the director of the Bombay office. Balan and his wife Rukmini would welcome him into their Bombay home on numerous visits during 1978–79, as if he was a relative visiting from Kerala. In short, Jose continued to cultivate friends as he did during his Madras days.

The officer ranks of Maldives Shipping vessels in those days were held by Philippines nationals. It was no secret that many Filipinos considered dog meat a delicacy. However, the crew was invariably local, mostly believers of Islam, and therefore would not even considering touching a dog. Trouble began looming when the vessel stopped at the port of Latakia in Syria, where one of the officers took a dog on board and kept it hidden from the crew.

The issue came to a boil when the ship was still in the high seas. One crew member spread the word that he had seen a dog, which must have been brought aboard for the officers to eat. The stand-off between the crew and the officers began to take on the proportions of a mutiny. The ship captain was advised by the South East Asia HQ in Bombay that the vessel should head out to Cochin, bypassing Bombay.

'I came to know of all this when I received an urgent call from Capt. Ricky. I had no doubt that Mujtaba was keeping a close tab. Clearly, as the dog was a stowaway, the Maldivians would have landed in big trouble, given the potential for international law to be interpreted by lawyers ever ready to get themselves involved. There was also the religious angle to consider as the officers had maintained the dog was a figment of the crew's imagination. This was payback time for me, to return one favour for the many that Maldives Shipping had thrown my way,' recalls Jose.

What followed was high drama. Jose boarded the ship as it was getting berthed, sprinting up the gangway. Around 2 a.m., Jose smuggled out the little Latakian stowaway dog, put him in the boot of his car and drove away at breakneck speed, fully knowing the repercussions that would follow if he were to get caught.

'I knew I had to clear the port premises before anyone noticed, so I pushed the accelerator as hard as I could. It was as if the car was being driven on auto-pilot! It stopped when I reached Thevara. I let the dog out near Thevara Church where it joined a group of strays. I could not risk taking it home as there was always a chance of being connected to the incident. The dog remained in the Thevara area for many years—my secret for many months, one that I kept for my Maldivian friends,' concludes Jose.

Those were the days Jose was game for any adventure, provided it offered a chance to shore up his reserves, given the vagaries that faced the seafood industry. It is not that Choice Canning was not functioning, but it was doing so without creating any real ripples. All the action was coming from the allied activities that Jose engaged in. One such escapade earned him the nickname of pattharwalla or one who deals in crushed rocks and gravel.

It all began with a telex that he received from his Maldives Shipping friends in Bombay around 1980–81, announcing that their government was looking for an agent to supply river sand and crushed stone gravel for an airport runway they were building back home. The requirement was 80,000 tonnes of river sand and 50,000 tonnes of gravel. They were looking for Indian agents to supply the same.

'While the river sand procurement was sewn up by someone else, I decided to throw in my hat in the ring for the gravel as I knew a few quarry owners in Kerala. In the months that followed, I was mostly involved in moving gravel from many parts of Kerala, through Cochin port, via the Maldives Shipping vessels. For almost a year, I felt my hair was gritty with gravel dust. While I was not physically carrying the load, there was no escaping the relentless dust particles,' recounts Jose.

His mother would keep asking him to wash his hair as soon as he returned home after a gruelling day at the port, having seen off yet another vessel filled with gravel! The local youth, some of them from the Gujarati community, coined the fitting new name for Jose—pattharwalla ('Gravel Man').

On 11 November 1981, Male International Airport, with an improved infrastructure, including a better runway, was officially inaugurated by President Muamoom Abdul Gayoom.

'I would take on the might of the Shipping Corporation of India during 1983–84 and come out the winner in the battle for spices. The markets were spread across the port cities of Aden in Yemen, Amman in Jordan, ports in Syria including

Latakia and the port of Djibouti on the other side of the Mediterranean. I would rule the Red Sea route for the next seven years and remain a shipping agent for the next twenty-five years,' sums up Jose.

The torch of passion for shipping first ignited by DP in Madras would go on to make a shippie out of Jose. He would keep falling back on this revenue stream whenever the vagaries of seafood industry wreaked damage on Choice Canning's revenue streams. Right through a good part of the next few decades, he would keep juggling the two verticals, one bailing out the other in the hour of need.

Sure, it was seafood export that got Jose to relocate to the US in the mid-1980s. But this began with shipping. True to nature, Jose would shift focus from shipping the moment it became apparent that the key to survival in the US would require the rediscovery of the 'shrimp king' in him, with loads of market savviness.

Sure, Maldives would never figure in his plans in the future. But it must be acknowledged that Jose's true voyage of life began with the connections he built from Maldives. A bulk of the wealth he earned till then came from anything but his chosen areas of trade. That streak in him would persist for a fairly long time. But the mother of all windfall gains was just around the corner when he would don the garb of what we later became familiar with, the release of Indiana Jones movies. Jose was destined to find his pot of gold in the distant African continent.

8

A MANDARIN DILEMMA

IN JOSE'S BOOK OF ACCOUNTS, IT HAS ALWAYS BEEN ABOUT balancing two sheets—seafood and shipping. Invariably, one would feed the other, each becoming a mode of sustenance when the other was under strain. It would be many years before seafood would emerge the clear winner, with shipping destined to play a supporting role. Yet, it was ultimately shipping that really made Jose the man he is today.

This voyage allowed him to be a part of the many changes the industry witnessed, including the Panamax vessels, the McLean era and containerized frozen cargo. In comparison, seafood, with little scope for new ventures, was no match for the exciting world of shipping that literally opened up the world to him. It was only much later, when the value-added aspect of seafood trade opened up, that he staked claim as a player in the food industry. That is when Jose started warming up to his family enterprise of marine goods exports.

Sreenivasan, his friend from Sumitomo Corporation, still remembers the day his first ship as agent docked at the Ernakulam wharf: 'I remember being told how he shared the agent's fee to get the show going. It was the Mother India Shipping Company. I watched him spend a sleepless night as he could not wait for the dawn. It was still dark outside; we all pushed off to Willingdon Island—Jose, his mother, other family members. He was like a young boy, jumping up and down, shouting out his victory call. At the age of twenty-four, he was on his way to conquer the world.'

In the months that followed, Jose fashioned himself as an entrenched shipping agent. Mentoring him were the trio of Capt. Menon, Capt. Ricky and Capt. Gopalan. The number of his friends in the shipping sector started swelling as he started allocating less time to the seafood business. Jose was a popular figure around Willingdon Island, having made his mark as a shippie at such a young age.

Then there was that pivotal development, which set off a chain of events that would signal to those willing to watch that all the stars were getting aligned in his favour. Till then, it was never his plan, nor did he have the expertise, in salvaging a ship.

Jose vividly recalls that rainy day in June 1981 when Capt. Varghese Kuruvilla, one of his recently acquired friends at the Cochin Port, invited him to a lunch meeting.

'Capt. Varghese confided in me that he was facing a problem; he thought I was the right person to handle it. Sometime ago, I received an SOS call saying there was a vessel drifting outside Cochin waters, all the way from Colombo. As dictated by the Maritime Act, the port authorities had towed and anchored the vessel, *New Mandarin*, in Cochin. The Chinese owners had abandoned the vessel, now the engine had a major breakdown and there were no funds available,' says Jose.

An agent is like the traditional husband of the vessel and takes care of fuel, food for the crew, water, also the repair of the vessel. Chowgule Shipping had abandoned this role as there was no one to reimburse them for expenses incurred. The cargo was of Malaysian origin, the captain was a Chinese national and the deck crew, Burmese.

None aboard could speak English, so the destination remained a mystery. Capt. Varghese asked me casually if I would be willing to take up the husbanding of *New Mandarin*,' Jose reminisces with a twinkle in his eye.

The first lien expected was ₹100 crore! Chowgule resigned and Jose, representing TeeJay Shipping, took over. The crew had been having a great time, using amenities such as air-conditioning, not to mention diesel-guzzling generators, unmindful of the cost. Their daily menu had pork, mutton, and beef. Paying for this extravaganza was the owner's responsibility.

'As I boarded the gangway of the ship, the captain, sensing trouble, wanted to know who I was. His fears proved right when I spelt out the new rules of engagement. Some of my cost-cutting measures included the limitation of generator use to four hours a day, a sharp ration on fuel consumption and a less rich menu. The crew recorded their protest by lighting firewood on the deck,' Jose recalls.

The incident made news, even hitting the headlines in a national newspaper, given the international context. To this day, Jose wonders why the reporter did not bother to investigate the story behind the ship getting into trouble. He attributes it to lazy reporting.

'There was a much bigger story there which went unreported. The diesel for the ship, the ration for the crew, and the daily ₹50,000 parking fee had piled up. Determined to find a solution to the *New Mandarin* problem, I invoked the provisions of international maritime law to send the crew home. I took the legal route and filed for a lien on the ship, as did the Chinese captain. The court proceedings were by then being reported by the local media,' he adds.

After much probing by the shipping ministry, it came to be known that the Sudanese government had purchased the Malaysian timber to make railway sleepers with World Bank's aid. It was established that Sudan Railway was the consignee of the cargo onboard.

Jose's continued association with the Gujarati trading community had led to him exporting tea to Khartoum. It panned out that he had a few connections in Sudan, including one with some nuns who were involved in missionary work in the interiors of the African nation.

In the meantime, the government machinery had started moving—slowly but quite steadily. A call was made from the Sudan Embassy in Bombay. Omar Khayyam, the Consulate General of Sudan, flew down to Kochi to meet Jose at Malabar Hotel.

The Sudanese government had so far spent $10 million in the search of the lost ship. They were relieved to learn that the ship had a new agent in Jose who was handling all matters. Finally, the Central government referred the case to Kochi.

'The Consulate General thanked me for husbanding and keeping *New Mandarin* and her cargo safe. He wanted to know if I could manage to deliver the ship's cargo to Sudan. However, gratitude alone was not a reward for the hassles I had faced and the cost incurred. I was brutally honest about the consequences the Sudanese government should be prepared for,' says Jose.

He then made a bold request, fully expecting it to be turned down. To his surprise, they agreed. Consequently, the Sudanese government made Jose a secondary representative with considerable powers to decide the fate of *New Mandarin*.

Once Jose was nominated an official representative of the Sudan Railway Ministry, it was documented proof that could be produced before the Kerala High Court. As a result, he had the first lien on the ship and he could deliver *New Mandarin's* freight to Khartoum.

The court verdict had gone in Jose's favour. Thereafter, things started gathering momentum. Almost immediately, a meeting was arranged between Jose and a minister of the Sudanese government. The full scope of the arduous task he had taken on was laid bare before Jose. First, it was established that as *New Mandarin* was immobile, it had to be towed. Then, the load had to be discharged from *New Mandarin* and then reloaded into smaller vessels.

Leveraging his prevailing association with Maldives Shipping, Jose went to Male. He requested them to send two empty vessels to Cochin to load cargo from *New Mandarin* and send it to Sudan. As the cost of carriage was to be borne by Sudanese government, Maldives Shipping was happy to send two vessels to Cochin.

Weighing in his favour was one thing—he had already been to Sudan in connection with his exports. He had even scoured the countryside for bus rides along with nuns hailing from Kerala, conversing with them in Malayalam. While that by itself did not mean much in the present context, it surely gave him immense confidence about the new assignment he was about to undertake, with an underlying sense of familiarity.

After all the high-seas drama along the Cochin coast, the actual voyage to Khartoum was so uneventful that it was almost an anti-climax. Finally, almost a year after Jose received that life-changing call from Capt. Varghese, the cargo of *New Mandarin* that started out from Port Klang near Kuala Lumpur was delivered to Sudan Railways.

'It gives me goosebumps even today to relive those glory days when the representatives of the Sudanese government invited me to London, where they maintained all the transaction details for the final settlement of *New Mandarin*. They paid me a fortune, way above what I had hoped for. I remember with absolute clarity—it was a Bank of Tokyo cheque for $800,000. It was an astronomical amount in those days!' Jose recounts, a sense of wonder lacing his words even after so many years.

'The Sudanese government team that met me said they owed me only $300,000 in fees. The additional $500,000 was a token of their huge appreciation for my initiative and enterprise in salvaging the cargo that was crucial to their infrastructure development,' he adds.

Jose's total expenditure, after settling all dues in Cochin Port and paying off the Chinese captain and crew, was around $200,000, leaving him with a windfall gain of $600,000! The *New Mandarin*, for all the heartache the vessel had caused him, had proved to be his jackpot, a bonanza that one could only have dreamt of. Yet, the *New Mandarin* story does not quite end there.

'When I returned from London, this white elephant, *New Mandarin*, was still docked at the port. As per the court ruling, the technical owner of the vessel was the Sudanese government, with me being the local representative. As I was the legally appointed Sudan Railways representative, I could do what I wanted,' Jose recites the story with a wistful sigh.

Jose began conferring with Capt. Jacob George, his friend in Cochin Port to find a feasible solution. The most obvious option was to take it the world's largest graveyards of ships in the world, the Alang Shipbreaking Yard in Bhavnagar, Gujarat. However, there was a curious problem weighing down the vessel in the Cochin waters. The *New Mandarin* had no engine!

In the interim, it was costing Jose an arm and a leg in wharfage charges. It took him six months to identify two things—a buyer for the ships valuable parts when stripped down for breaking and a viable location near Cochin to break the ship.

'We got in touch with Kaliappa Chettiar, a metal trader in the Broadway market in the city. Capt. George helped me in convincing Chettiar about the valuable metal parts available in a ship such as the one we had with us. Once he took stock of the ship's interiors, he realized there was a fortune to be made by stripping the vessel of parts made of brass, steel, aluminium and iron. We struck a deal for ₹2.8 million,' he says, narrating it as if it happened only the other day.

Jose and his friend had already identified a small boat repair yard that was engaged in building boats in the nearby Vypeen mainland. They used tugs hired from Cochin port to tow the vessel to the mainland where it was beached on the sandbanks in front of a huge crowd that had never in their lifetime seen a beached ship!

He heaved a sigh of satisfaction as he was done with the *New Mandarin* for good this time. The success of this operation transformed Jose into a very confident person willing to undertake any challenge connected with the ocean—right from representing ship owners to salvaging ships.

9

WILLINGDON ISLAND

THE MISSISSIPPI RIVER HAS A LIFE OF ITS OWN AND PLAYS THE central character in Mark Twain's *The Adventures of Huckleberry Finn*. Similarly, Willingdon Island played a critical role in the life of young Jose as he started carving out a name for himself in the world of shipping and seafood industries.

The history of Willingdon Island and Taj Malabar is closely interwoven. In 1919, Lord Willingdon was appointed Governor of the Madras Presidency. It was decided to dredge a channel from the open seas into what eventually became the Cochin Harbour encompassing the gulf between Cochin, Mattanchery and other mainland segments like Vypeen, with Sir Robert C. Bristow as the engineer-in-charge.

By 1929, the dredged sand and other materials resulted in the formation of the 900-acre island. It was the Maharajah of Cochin who suggested in 1933 that the newly formed reclamation land be named after Lord Willingdon. It soon became apparent that a hotel was essential if passenger ships were to call at Cochin Harbour and so the task of building one was yet again entrusted to Sir Bristow.

What began in 1935 as Willingdon Island Hotel, run by Spencer's & Co, was later renamed Malabar Hotel and came to be the main attraction for the wealthy making a stop in Cochin. Before the Taj Group procured the licence from Cochin Port Trust in 1984 to run Malabar Hotel by renaming it Taj Malabar, the licence had changed hands twice.

In 1954, Dominic Joseph, along with his brother Thomas Joseph, won the bid from Cochin Port Trust for the running of the Malabar Hotel which had been run by Spencer & Co. until then. This arrangement was for ten years until 1964 and this was extended for another five years till 1969. There is some intrigue surrounding how the fifteen-year tenure of the Casino Group ended and the licence to run the hotel changed hands in favour of D.C. Johar in 1969.

In 1969, Dominic Joseph's bid was the highest, yet the contract was awarded to D.C. Johar, the second-highest bidder. The Malabar Hotel was considered the premium hotel of Cochin and heads of state are lodged there. However, when the President of Seychelles visited Cochin during the time when Malabar Hotel was under D.C. Johar's lease, the visiting head of state was lodged in Casino Hotel.

D.C. Johar got the lease of Malabar Hotel transferred to Taj mid-term for the remainder of the lease. It was at this time that Taj built the new block and initially it was said Taj were granted a lease tenure for ninety-nine years by Cochin Port Trust. Later, it was understood that the lease tenure of ninety-nine years was not approved by the government of India (GoI) and in reality the lease tenure was restricted to thrity years.

By then, Willingdon Island had emerged as the hub of all international trade out of Kerala. While Cochin Port facilitated international cargo movement, most of the feeder activities were taken care of by the goods trains at the Cochin Harbour Terminus, colloquially called the 'Island' station.

A significant part of the tea trade was routed out of the Island, as was the bulk movement of quite a few spices, apart from seafood exports. Cochin port continued to lord over the lion's share of trade out of Kerala till the D.P. World container port terminal at Vallarpadam unseated her from the throne.

It was not surprising that Jose would be enchanted by the dynamics of the shipping sector as it offered more allure and glamour than shrimp exports ever could. Right from the 1980s, heading into the new millennium, the shipping industry witnessed so many positive developments that someone like Jose, with his proximity to Willingdon Island, was bound to find himself hugely attracted to it.

Jose began making the Island his base for all activities in the 1979–80 period, he was enjoying the heydays of his association with Maldives Shipping. The Taj Group was not yet in the picture, as the iconic Island Hotel was then called Malabar Hotel.

In a sense, it could be argued that the Taj Group inherited Jose along with Malabar Hotel in 1985 because he would continue to mount many of his offensives and retreats from that prime property on Willingdon Island.

If you ask Jose why, he would simply say he needed that touch of class to ward off his debtors as much as to impress his future clients! No surprise there as the Island was where all the export houses that mattered had their warehouses. Quite a few of them, like Jose, who had turned regular exporters or shipping agents, also had their offices there.

The connection goes way beyond the fact that his first corporate office was based out of Ninan's Cold Storage building on the fifth crossroad, situated fairly close to the

Ernakulam wharf and Cochin Port Trust. That address was not worth a big shout-out by itself as the building was essentially a warehouse for frozen goods.

It was Ninan's cold storage building that gave Jose an address, a valid calling card. It was this address that made him an integral part of the bustling commercial hub that was Cochin in those days, with Willingdon Island functioning as the gateway to the vast expanse of Kerala.

Jose was determined to grow beyond the confines of being just another seafood exporter by going full steam ahead into the shipping business. When even that was not enough to keep him fully occupied, he would be off the starting block the moment he chanced upon a new adventure. The *New Mandarin* venture had vetted his appetite for more such forays. That exploit had led Jose to associate more closely with Capt. George, where they jointly owned a deep-sea fishing vessel. His association with Maldives Shipping had pushed Jose into a zone where he could do no wrong while chasing after opportunities that were not even vaguely connected to his core strength in seafood exports.

It was in the early 1980s that Capt. George called Jose about some serious money to be made. It was not unknown that the Oil and Natural Gas Corporation (ONGC) was planning to initiate preliminary exploration for oil and gas off Ambalapuzha coast, south of Alappuzha. Capt. George had been told that ONGC was looking to salvage some large pipes that had been lost in sea as a storm had struck the region.

'I told Capt. George we should give it a shot as the senior managers of ONGC were desperate to retrieve the floating pipes, probably because they wanted to avoid the potential bad publicity. We volunteered help and took off in our vessel, accompanied by a few other boats we hired for the salvage operation. It took us almost a week, but we recovered about 200 pipes of 1 metre diameter that were floating around in the sea. It was no easy task, but our effort was well rewarded. ONGC paid us ₹2.5 million,' says Jose with a glint of satisfaction in his eyes.

Things were looking so good for Jose that his mother decided it was the right time for him to get married. He was quite the eligible bachelor, hailing from a reputed family, heading a renowned corporate group, making loads of money, perhaps the one drawback being he had no college education.

'One day my mother declared to all those who would listen that it was time for me to get married. I was quite busy with multiple engagements but when she started lining up girls from suitable families for me to meet. I started visiting them one after the other,' recalls Jose.

The best part, he remembers, is after a long drive and going through the tedium of the traditional pennukaanal ceremony, he would tell his mother that he liked the girl. Pennukaanal is all about a prospective groom calling on a prospective bride under the strict guidance of elders with the stated purpose of reaching an agreement of marriage between the two families.

'I must have agreed to marry about a dozen girls as I wanted to get this ceremony over with so that I could get on with my activities without my mother chasing after me all the time. Yet, she kept pointing out shortcomings of every prospective bride's father, mother or some close relative and kept shooting down each proposal,' remembers Jose with a chuckle.

Elizabeth was the fourteenth girl Jose called on as per the wishes of his mother. They found each other acceptable as a future couple. More importantly, his mother found no fault with her family that hailed from the same district, Ernakulam. As was the custom, he asked her a few perfunctory questions, which she promptly answered.

'I remember asking about her education. She said she was a graduate. Luckily, she did not ask about mine, probably because she knew that was one question that should not be asked to spare me the blushes. My mother as also my many sisters seemed pleased with her. However, things almost took a dramatic turn, about which I would learn much later when she told her father about a rumour she had heard, resulting in Elizabeth getting cold feet,' adds Jose.

It was a rumour that reached her via her collegemates that Jose used to invite girls aboard the many ships he handled in the Cochin port. Worse, she was told that later those girls would disappear! Luckily, her father reassured her it was nothing but a wild rumour with no basis in truth!

They married in September 1982.

In course of time, Jose came to the conclusion that Maldives Shipping had no plans to move on with the technological advancements that came into the sea transportation world—containerization. Consequently, in his ambition to keep in step with the emerging trends in shipping, Jose started searching for ship owners who had containerized vessels for movement of cargo. True to form, he put his foot on the pedal so that there was no time lost.

It was not as if containerized cargo came as a surprise—a peek into the past developments in and around Cochin port would make this abundantly clear. Things were undergoing a transformation at the Cochin Port. The Ernakulam wharf that used to be the hub of all imports and exports at Cochin port, began facing serious competition from the Mattancherry wharf, which would start calling the shots for the next two decades. This passing of the mantle also gave the opportunity for a few enterprising youngsters to get their toe-hold in the business of freight handling that was till then the monopoly of a few. Jose would be one of them.

Willingdon Island began withering away as Kerala's primary hub of commercial activity when it got hit on multiple fronts. The first nail in its coffin was the commissioning of the Cochin International Airport in Nedumbassery in 1999. Things went further south for the island when the first phase of the Vallarpadam container terminal got going in 2011 with DP World as the operator.

The writing on the wall became clear when the Cochin Harbour Terminus, that once used to be the final destination of many trains till the mid-1970s, became commercially unviable with the commissioning of the Vallarpadam terminal. The Harbour Terminus, that was a major railway station, Kerala's answer to Victoria Terminus in Bombay, stopped dead in its tracks.

There is no argument that Willingdon Island is now a ghost town, the only activity there limited to the few cement factories, apart from the Indian Oil facility. Over 800 residential quarters belonging to the port, railways and the customs department have been demolished. The few that have survived are lying vacant as there is hardly any life there. Even the naval quarters empty out when schools shut for holidays. For Jose, however, his heydays in shipping for almost a good decade were irrevocably enmeshed with the fortunes of the island which was a source of great energy for him.

'Our life revolved around activities that began and ended in the island. Thus, all my engagements, whether it was with Maldives Shipping, Ceylon Shipping or many of my adventures like the one involving *New Mandarin* were based out of Willingdon. I had my office there on Ninan's Cold Storage building from 1979 to 1990, which was perhaps the most happening period of my life in terms of the exciting situations I encountered. Willingdon Island is the place that moulded me into who I am today. The island will always be a part of me,' reiterates Jose.

Willingdon Island continued to serve Jose as a platform to mount many battles, at the same time doubling up as a place of retreat for him when facing reverses. Playing an equally critical role in many of these manoeuvres is the majestic Malabar Hotel, situated on the tip of Willingdon Island, majestically overseeing all the traffic along the Cochin Harbour.

The island would continue to hold a special place in his heart, even after he relocated to the US. The sundry suppliers to whom Jose once owed payment were invited to Taj Malabar for a grand feast, followed by a speech that got them to agree to a deferred payment plan. Such capers from the past may never happen again! That is the magic of the place that Jose carries in his heart.

10

CEYLON CONNECTION

IN 1983, INDIA LIFTED THE PRUDENTIAL CRICKET WORLD CUP at Lord's in London.

Jose managed to get almost the entire Indian team to come to Kochi to play a charity match there. The teams were led by two Indian captains of the time. Kapil Dev XI squared off against Sunil Gavaskar XI. Only Jose could have managed to get the best names in Indian cricket, including Ravi Shastri, Sachin Tendulkar and the rest, to play in Kochi, which was at that time not known for hosting high-profile cricket matches. Jose's shipping business was at a crossroads in 1984, and the charity match was a welcome relief.

As Maldives Shipping continued to limit its portfolio to bulk carrier, Jose realized the time was ripe for him to find a shipping line that engaged in the container cargo trade. Thus began his exploration for a new shipping line.

'I started receiving information about Ceylon Shipping Corporation, the national shipping line of Sri Lanka which was efficiently and professionally managed compared to some of the other national shipping lines in the region. In Colombo,

I had a dear friend, Faizal Hashim, whom I used to call "Machan". He set up meetings for me with the brass of Ceylon Shipping. I soon travelled to Colombo,' recalls Jose.

Ceylon Shipping, with its headquarters in Bristol Street, housed the decision-makers for container cargo. The line-up included the general manager, operations manager, divisional heads of Europe, Far East and the Middle East. All these key positions were held by Lankans.

The shipping line had both mid-sized vessels with 400 containers as well as large vessels with around 1,500 container capacity. Everything suited Jose, but unfortunately he failed to make any headway with the managers.

He knew there was only one person who could bypass the entire boardroom and clinch the agency in Jose's favour. That was the chairman of Ceylon Shipping, Mr Caspers. Like a sleuth, Jose started tracking Caspers, studying his habits, likes and dislikes.

He soon came to know that Caspers frequently visited Singapore. That was the chance Jose was waiting for. He too made a trip to Singapore at the same time, even booking himself at the same hotel as Ceylon Shipping's chairman.

All his efforts were coming to nought as he never could 'casually bump into him or strike up a conversation as if by chance.' He had almost given up, when on the last day, which was a Sunday, he spotted Caspers heading out to attend the morning mass in a nearby church in downtown Singapore. Realizing this could be his last chance, Jose too followed him to church.

'I knelt next to the chairman who was praying and after allowing him a decent interval to pray, I introduced myself. I said I was a shipping agent from Kochi, India. As he introduced himself, I exclaimed it was the plan of God that we should meet in Singapore, and that too, in a church. I confided that I had a presentation to make to him about Lankan vessels making their entry at Indian ports. He seemed impressed with my insight about the opportunities Indian ports could offer his shipping line.'

It is anybody's guess whether Caspers believed it was a chance meeting he had with a wannabe Indian shipping agent for his line in Singapore. Yet, not one to let go of such an advantage, as soon as he returned to Kochi, Jose contacted Caspers' secretary and fixed a meeting in Colombo. It was a cakewalk as Jose had an offer that the Lankans simply could not refuse and said he was ready for the first Sri Lankan vessel.

The *Lanka Mudhitha*, with a carrying capacity of 105 containers, had to load the cargo from Kochi for European as well as Middle-eastern destinations before loading it onto larger vessels at Colombo. As the *Lanka Mudhitha* shuttled between Kochi and Colombo, the exporters in his hometown began depending on Ceylon Shipping.

This new status meant Jose was now required to divide his time between Colombo and Kochi. Always open to new opportunities and quick to make friends, Jose started becoming a familiar face in the Colombo shipping circles, as he got busy cultivating new contacts. After Caspers' tenure, the chairmanship of Ceylon Shipping was bestowed on Lionel Fernando, a civil servant.

Within a short while, Fernando became Jose's trusted friend. In less than a year, Jose had established contacts across the spectrum, including the political class of the island country. His stature in Colombo was such that he was seen more as an advisor to Ceylon Shipping than as one of its many agents across the globe.

'As life progressed, I began moving in the exalted circles of the Sri Lankan government. I was able to count the Minister of Trade and Shipping, Lalit Athulathmudali, as a friend and through him, a few ministers in the Cabinet, including Prime Minister R. Premadasa! Things came to such a pass that Ceylon Shipping would not take a major decision without consulting me,' says Jose as he travels back in time.

His relationship with Fernando was so close that he started staying with him during his sudden visits to Colombo. Jose says he is not exaggerating when he says that the local trading community used to tease him as if he was the de-facto owner of Ceylon Shipping.

In hindsight, it was this proximity with the Sri Lankan company that paved the way for the most important stepping stone in Jose's life—the decision to make his new home in the US. However, that alone would have come to nought if he had totally abandoned his ties with the island nation when he got on what would prove to be a heady trip in 1983 with the ultimate name in world shipping—the US Lines.

That was the year most Indians cherish as the one that saw the nation lift the Prudential Cricket World Cup at Lord's, London. Jose had even better reasons to remember it. His dream run with US Lines would last from then for another two years, till 1985.

11

US LINES

JOSE ALWAYS BELIEVED IN HAVING MULTIPLE IRONS IN THE fire as it was always his experience that many of them would go cold. Though he went flat out to get himself selected onboard the US Lines bandwagon as its only south India associate, Jose made sure he kept intact his ties with Ceylon Shipping for many more years to come.

The rise and fall of the US Lines is also the rise and fall of Malcolm McLean. He was an American, celebrated as the father of the container shipping industry worldwide, and had started SeaLand, one of the biggest shipping lines that controlled global trade in those days. The other company operating in the same league was the American President Line.

The American President Line had a carrying capacity of 2,500–3,000 containers per ship. The shipping circles were stunned when Malcolm left SeaLand to start US Lines, with the vision of building some of the largest ships, for which he joined hands with South Korean companies to build these new vessels. He collaborated with Korean shipyard and came up with a design where a ship could carry 4,400 containers. It was a revolutionary step and invited much criticism from other shipping majors.

Malcolm took the world of shipping by storm when he brought out twelve vessels, all with the capacity to carry 4,400 containers.* They were fitted with low-powered engines to reduce the speed of the vessel, thus saving fuel consumption. It went eastwards, around the whole world in seventy-two days, covering Japan, the Pacific, Panama Canal, the US east coast and the Suez Canal.

During the mid-1980s when Malcolm came up with this idea, the price of crude oil was quite high. Hence, his idea was to outflank his competition by running economically capable vessels in terms of fuel consumption. Based on this, he named this service Econ. These vessels were designed and planned to go towards the east and around the world in just seventy-two days.

Every aspiring shipping agent in India wished to represent the US Lines. Many of them applied, as did Jose. Based on his personal drive, Jose was convinced he stood a very good chance. Though Jose knew there were a number of established companies in the fray as his competitors, almost all of them with far better financial credentials, yet he was confident that it would be him, Jose Thomas, and not the others who would be shortlisted to represent US Lines in India.

To the surprise of all, twenty-nine-year-old Jose did make the cut! He went to Cranford, a township in New Jersey,

---

* Alexander Hammond, 'Malcom McLean: Truck Driver, Entrepreneur, Billionaire McLean designed stackable shipping containers and offered transport prices that were 25 percent lower than the competition', Fee Stories, 11 May 2019, fee.org/articles/malcolm-mclean-truck-driver-entrepreneur-billionaire/;

14 miles southwest of Manhattan where, apart from him, only the elites were invited. There were many aspiring representatives from the Indian subcontinent. He had his first presentation which went well and US Lines' head of operations, Charley Early, asked him why he was not pitching for the whole of India. What clinched the agency for Jose was his ability to convince the US Lines team why Indian operations were always split between north and south India. It was Jose's pitch that he was the ideal man for south India.

The top management of US Lines took an immediate shine to him, probably as his aggressive stance reflected their own approach to life in the fast lane. The result? Jose was tentatively identified as the shipping agent of US Lines from south India while another big name in Indian shipping became its representative for the rest of India.

It was a great moment. A sense of hope and achievement started seeping in at the Choice HQ. The final announcement was to be made later. He went on a celebratory family trip to Ooty. The next day, he eagerly called Charley Early's assistant and was stunned by what he heard over the phone. Charley had succumbed to a massive stroke the previous night!

Jose was blindsided by this shocking news as he was almost certain that the curtains had been pulled over his dream as Charley had been his single-point contact in US Lines. With Charley gone, he could not have been faulted for getting that sinking feel in the pit of his stomach that fate had once again conspired to deal him a harsh blow.

'I was prepared for the worst as other senior officers of the US Lines who interviewed me did not seem too convinced by my arguments for appointing me as their dedicated agent in south India. Therefore, imagine my surprise and overwhelming joy when I got the official appointment letter as the sole agent for US Lines in south India!' he says, reliving what was to be a major milestone in his life story.

Appointing him as an agent, as Jose learned at a later stage, came about as Charley had written a note prior to his death to McLean, highlighting the potential Jose could provide for US Lines to penetrate the south Indian market effectively. Even though some of the officials had a different opinion, Charley Early's recommendation clearly carried weight.

'I learned all about high living and the corporate lifestyle from my engagement with US Lines. I was coached by some of the most qualified specialists in the etiquettes of hosting parties. From getting the table manners right to the correct way of dressing and speaking, they completely overhauled my approach to life, in a sense my entire personality,' says Jose, who then felt the world literally was at his feet.

He recalls the first time he was asked to host a customer get-together on behalf of US Lines by David Harper, the India head. He was told explicitly not to tighten the purse strings. One must remember, those were the days when a food bill of ₹500 per head was perceived as astronomical.

Jose felt this was an ideal opportunity to showcase his negotiating skills by diligently paring down the expenses while offering a ten-course dinner. The newbie could not hide his sense of anticipation about the glowing tributes he was sure to receive after submitting a total under $1,000 against the approved sum of $1,500.

'Imagine my surprise when the head of accounts from Dubai blasted me for cutting corners and scrounging on the approved amount. The logic was, had I spent up to the approved limits, the potential customers of the company would have gone back with an even bigger image of the hosts,' says Jose, admitting that that was the benchmark he started setting thereafter.

What followed were days of wining and dining in the finest hotels around the world. Jose, as a representative of US Lines, transformed himself into a desi American. The manner in which he conducted himself in public—the way he spoke, the diction, intonation and accent, all changed.

He was never a wealthy person in the conventional sense, though the family had considerable assets. The one thing that set him apart was his uncanny ability not only to identify opportunities, but to go chasing after them single-mindedly, despite the risks involved. There was always the possibility that things could go wrong anytime but that was one risk that always had to be factored in, and over time, Jose started mastering this aspect.

US Lines redefined his aspiration levels. So, it was like the ground was swept from under his feet when the global crash of crude price set off a chain of events in 1985.

The fall of US Lines was mainly due to the competition-running vessels that could deliver cargo faster than US Lines. This resulted in cargo owners not supporting US Lines which resulted in their cash flow getting depleted and finally leading Malcolm to file for bankruptcy. Ironically, its unique selling point had become the reason for its decline.

It was a crippling blow because Jose barely had enough time to savour the feeling of emerging as the south India associate of US Lines after a gruelling race that involved many aspirants. He had started making big plans involving his entire family's future. He thought he had finally made it big yet his dreams had been snuffed out by developments completely beyond his control.

It was an experience that he would later liken to his personal Titanic experience—one that left a sinking feeling in the pit of his stomach. He was swamped by a sense of gloom as all his dreams of making it big as the shipping agent for US Lines in south India lay shattered.

'The Econ vessels were the hallmark of the McLean model and formed the foundation of the entire fleet of US Lines. Unfortunately, for the shipping behemoth, when the fuel price fell in 1985, what vanished into thin air was his ability to offer low pricing to his customers on account of having access to vessels with low fuel consumption. What came crashing down were the aspirations of hundreds of employees and associates. I had the misfortune to be one of them,' says Jose, with a wistful sigh.

This was one of the biggest shocks of Jose's life—losing US Lines. Not because it was his fault, but as he said, it was destiny. Fate had dealt another cruel blow. However, Jose realized he could not afford to wallow in self-pity for long. By now, a veteran of quite a few lost causes, Jose decided it would be far wiser to start focusing on the takeaways from his association with US Lines. He decided to mask his setback by putting on a show.

Jose set up Club Choice—a private club inside his corporate office—where he entertained his creditors more than anyone else. Some people found this investment on the club a real gimmick for Jose to hide some facts on his financial condition. He says that was not his intention—it was to build up confidence in people.

'I acquired the first BMW in Kochi soon after the biggest setback in my life. The only red BMW car in Kerala, parked outside my office, was as much a statement to those scrutinizing my financial health as it was to unassuming people, attracted by that car. What did it matter to them if I was broke or not?' quips Jose allowing an insight into how the grooming he received from US Lines altered his philosophy on life.

One man who was impressed by his BMW was Malayalam film actor, Mammootty. The other person who was mighty impressed by that car was a young school boy who would later marry Jose's eldest daughter, Anna.

Then he did the unthinkable for someone whose life was lying in ruins. He decided to tap into his meagre funds and go on a world tour along with his friend Capt. Jeff!

Says Capt. Jeff, originally from Tirunelveli in Tamil Nadu, who still spends a few days every year with his good friend Jose, a good thirty-seven years after they went on that world tour, 'It was a spur of the moment idea and we took off from Chennai. The trip which lasted twenty-two days saw us touch down in Singapore, Tokyo, Los Angeles, Chicago, Cleveland and New York before we landed back in Chennai. It was probably while we had halted in New York that Jose got the idea that it would make sense for him to reposition Choice as an American company.'

That may have been a spontaneous decision taken by a young man enamoured by the Big Apple. Jose, instead of forgetting this idea once they were back in India, nurtured it over the next two years before taking the plunge with his wife and kids to start a fresh innings in the US.

12

THE IMMIGRANT

IT WAS IN 1987 THAT JOSE MOVED TO THE US WITH THE AIM of starting his life from scratch. But the seeds of this major step in life were sown during the world tour he undertook with his friend Capt. Jeff in 1985.

'We reached New York and checked into Marriott World Trade Centre which also came down later with the 9/11 terror strike in 2001. We went visiting all the iconic destinations in and around Manhattan, and then returned to gaze up at the twin towers. I wondered aloud what it would be like to have an office there. Soon, this idea began growing in mind to almost an obsession, which I shared with Jeff,' confides Jose.

He was not sure how Jeff would respond. To Jose's surprise, he said it was a good idea, encouraged him to plan his next phase of life in the US. The fact is Jeff realized how much Jose was missing his high-flying days that came with being a part of the US Lines family. On his return to Kochi, Jose straightaway plunged into planning his eventual relocation to the US soil. Luckily for him, he found a willing partner in the Sri Lankan government.

His daughter Priya was over two years old and his son, Thomas one, when Jose decided to leave for America with his young wife and two toddlers. America seemed so warm and welcoming. There was no dearth of opportunities. It did not take too long for him to decide that Choice had to remain in the US no matter what he had to go through to achieve this goal.

Suddenly he thought of his relations with Ceylon Shipping in Colombo. He called Chairman Fernando and moved the idea of Ceylon Shipping entering Trans-Atlantic trade line which they never had. His idea was to get Ceylon Shipping involved and get himself appointed as their agent in USA.

After many trips to Colombo, discussions, submissions and deliberations, Ceylon Shipping Lines decided to sign a Connecting Carrier Agreement with many operators servicing the North Atlantic trade lane. 'This was a big turn in my life', says Jose.

Jose started the painstaking process by building a case before Lionel Fernando why Ceylon Shipping should look beyond Europe, Japan and Far East for trade. He convinced him the time was ripe for the island nation to start a direct shipping route to the US. The seeds of such an ambitious plan that were sown by Jose did not take long to yield results.

'I was summoned for a presentation of this project before Prime Minister of Sri Lanka R. Premadasa. He was impressed by what I said we could achieve in the US and gave his consent. Ceylon Shipping gave me the mandate to scout for an office in the US, study the market and so on. Soon I was shuttling between Colombo and New York on behalf of the Lankans. Thus, when I landed with my family in New York, it was with the mandate to start this shipping service. Seafood was nowhere in the picture,' Jose opens up.

The Sri Lankan national line supported his plan all the way and empowered him to start the service with full confidence. So that is what Jose did: he opened an office in New York for Ceylon Shipping.

'I started the New York office in 19, Rector Street, in 1987. The Ceylon Shipping head office had allocated $50,000 for setting the US office. Thus was born CeyLion Shipping. For me it was like a rebound after the US Lines episode. It was lavish; I hired big, even bought three cars. It was like I was putting together a smaller version of US Lines in New York under the banner of the Sri Lankan national carrier,' says Jose as he hits the rewind button.

His exceptional connections in Colombo notwithstanding, Sri Lanka was not exactly known at that time for its political stability. Tamil militancy was gathering momentum; the threat of violence was always a reality. As a result, government policies were always in a flux with no guarantee that there would be continuity in the existing economic activities.

Sri Lanka's US strategy began being questioned due to a combination of factors, financial viability being the foremost of them. At another level, Tamil separatist movement that had been gathering momentum for many years, had begun to get out of control. The resentment that had been building over years about undue Indian influence was reaching a flashpoint.

As shipping was among the Island country's major revenue streams, winds of change started sweeping this sector. By 1990, the financial viability of the American venture came under scrutiny. By 1991, they pulled the plug on the US office.

Though Jose's engagement with CeyLion Shipping began in 1987, virtually flagging off his stint in the US, it continued till 1991. But he had started revisiting his seafood contacts in the US by 1988. In short, it took him only a year to decide that the time was ripe for him to do unto Ceylon Shipping what he once did with Maldives Shipping—look at options.

Thus, while continuing to hold on to CeyLion Shipping, he fell back on his mainstay, seafood exports. The US was already his primary overseas market and he decided it was time for him to establish an office there. He had for some time been consumed by dark thoughts about middlemen eating into his American profits.

His logic was quite simple: it was these brokers who lived off the spoils they earned from the traders who called the shots, who pocketed the real profits, got to live luxuriously in Taj Malabar. Meanwhile, the local exporters had to pander to their whims and fancies to even get their audience. Jose swore to make it his mission to alter this reality.

He realized if he could directly connect with the buyer in the US, by cutting out the middleman, then both the exporter and the importer stood to substantially increase their margins. Understandably, the initial period was fraught with trouble with regard to former friends who sold his products in the US. It was an uphill task.

13

BUILDING BLOCKS

MOST PEOPLE WOULD WEIGH THE PROS AND CONS, EVEN pause and ponder about the what-ifs and why-nots before starting a new venture. They would turn doubly cautious when the new vertical is totally unrelated to what they are familiar with. These rules rarely applied to Jose.

One only has to take a cursory glance at the multiple diversification attempts made by him to understand this. It was as if he was deliberately avoiding a fate which was right from the beginning—a future intertwined with the seafood sector.

Jose, till date entrenched in seafood and shipping activities, decided it was worth his time and effort to get into the totally unrelated field of construction. It was like a deep dive into turbulent waters as the fund flow dynamics of residential units were completely alien to him.

Curiously, the seed of this idea to get into residential apartments came as a flash of inspiration to Jose while he was in New York. After a regular day's work at his downtown New York office, he had reason to visit midtown New York.

It had been a year then since he had settled down there, but the to-and-fro travel by the subway had so far left no chance to visit this upmarket residential section of the Big Apple.

Standing before the Empire State Building there, he admired the statuesque skyscrapers, the signature architecture, and the spectacular designs. The residents moved in and out with elegance. It appeared as if this part of the city was all about people living in a world of their own.

Well-groomed men and fashionable women moved in and out of glass elevators and decorated lobbies and stepped in or out of chauffeured limousines while some even drove their luxury cars. Something clicked in his mind.

He started pondering over an idea that could turn into the proverbial pot of gold. He wondered if he could replicate one such building in Kochi? He could hardly control his excitement! Soon, he was planning his next move, though he had to wait till his next trip to Kochi a month later.

Once in Kochi, he called a meeting with his senior managers and mooted the idea of taking baby steps into the world of construction. He was crestfallen as everyone started arguing against it, saying the spacious and sprawling Kochi left no scope for community living. However, one of his nephews encouraged him.

Before flying back to the US, he contacted an architect who incidentally did not have any idea about constructing a high-rise building. Yet, he was game and thus it was decided in 1987 that Choice would go in for the first of its kind high-rise building of a luxury apartments. An isolated parcel of land was identified in Vyttila, now the busiest location in the entire state.

The basic idea was to construct an opulent building with ninety-six apartments with all the modern amenities such as lush green gardens, large lobbies, spacious corridors, a swimming pool, clubs, and dedicated corners as children's play area. There were contractors and site men appointed. Work soon commenced.

While Jose was happy with the execution of the plan, he realized the picture was far from rosy at the grassroots level. The market was cold to the new concept and the message was loud and clear. The naysayers started mocking the venture saying the land was available in plenty for individual houses, so why should anyone settle for one part of a building. The upshot was—nobody wanted to buy an apartment.

Thus, even as the building reached the third floor, not a single apartment had been sold as the traditional Keralite continued to shun the concept of community living. All the brochures lay unanswered, despite frantic efforts at marketing, no sale resulted. Soon, the venture started running out of capital.

That was when Jose started thinking of the Indians abroad who knew only too well the benefits of community living. And they had surplus money. He decided to advertise in the Indian newspapers in the US, which was read by Malayali doctors. A senior executive was appointed in the US exclusively to market the apartment complex. The advertisements appeared, the marketing executive began making calls, and to his dismay, there was still no response.

By the weekend, a few days after publishing the advertisements, the phone began to ring and enquiries started coming in. A Malayali doctor living in Texas was the first to sign the sale deed. Taking a cue from this, Jose held road shows in various cities where a receptive Malayali community started buying the apartments in Kochi, based on the information provided in the US.

A few flats were thus booked from the US. Still, there was no way the project could succeed unless there was interest back home in Kochi where the multi-storeyed residential complex was being built. Jose was under tremendous pressure, being heavily strapped on the liquidity front.

'I had to go for short-term borrowings. But that is only one side of the story. It is out of desperation that many of my projects have undergone magical transformation. It was the same case with the 40-storeyed, 137-metre-tall Choice Paradise commissioned in 2012. It still remains one of the tallest residential buildings in south India. This time round, it was the most unlikely person you can imagine who bailed me out,' says Jose, striking an enigmatic note.

It was none other than the charismatic cricketing legend, the Haryana Hurricane, who virtually opened the floodgates of bookings of the hitherto unsold flats, barring a few units which were booked by Keralites based out of the US. It was that unexpected yorker from Kapil Dev that turned the sceptics of Kochi into believers of the virtues of Choice Paradise!

Jose invited the who's who of the city for a get-together at his resort-like corporate headquarters to launch Choice Paradise. The guest of honour was the Indian cricketing legend, Kapil Dev, who was at the pinnacle of his career, wooed by corporate India and the film world, feted by the nation, with the Padma Bhushan on its way, having already been conferred the Padma Shri.

'We began our friendship when Kapil visited Kochi with other cricketers to play an exhibition match in the mid-1980s that was sponsored by us. It was but natural that I would share with him my predicament, of sitting on dozens of unsold premium flats and at the same time strapped of cash due to an almost absent liquidity, ahead of the event. He knew I was pinning much hope on him doing a star turn for me,' recalls Jose with a fond smile that mirrored his genuine affection for Kapil.

What transpired was not unlike that stunning catch he produced to get rid of Vivian Richards in the 1983 World Cup. What he did immediately reversed Jose's luck as an aspiring builder. Kapil unlocked the floodgates in his typical style, by handing over a cheque to Jose saying he would be buying the first flat. Each and every person present was taken by surprise!

Kapil's impromptu gesture acted like a clarion call and within the next hour, the sales counter witnessed what Jose describes, perhaps with a slight exaggeration, a charge by the well-heeled citizens of the city, to get a flat where Kapil would be one of the residents, at least occasionally.

'Soon enough, we were flooded with calls and the sales team were converting a good number of those calls. It was like rain falling on parched land. There was no looking back after that. Later, I asked Kapil whether he really wanted to own a flat in Kochi. He said not really, but it was his genuine response to bail out a friend, and that he would figure out what to do with the flat later after he had bought it. I told him he had done more than enough by that single gesture and tore that cheque in front of him,' says Jose, with a wistful smile.

To this day, whenever they get together, Jose teases Kapil, saying he would have made a neat profit had he kept the flat. 'I know he would have made a good profit but it was generous warmth that we witnessed that day, a sincere effort to help a friend in need,' says Jose.

At one point, Choice Paradise was written off by many as the Ministry of Environment issued a stop order citing various issues. Everybody had then expected Jose to abandon the project. But instead of stopping the construction at the eighteenth-floor level, he decided to keep building.

His plan was to see if the authorities would dare to pull down all 40 floors. The bluff worked and the project was given the green signal. The entire city was captivated when he landed on the helipad in a chopper with Malayalam film star Mohanlal. Jose's friendship with Lal had just begun to bloom. It would be another turning point in Jose's life.

It was pure magic. Choice apartment projects were much sought-after, with prospective buyers coming from all over Kerala, many of them non-resident Indians. He made a loud statement with Choice Paradise, which was then the tallest building in south India. It was a luxury apartment spread over acres of land with every possible amenity available in the country, with another first—a helipad! Interestingly, he kept mixing things up, by offering upmarket villa projects right after the vertical residences.

Jose developed seven properties in his home state, all except one in Kochi, the other in the state capital Thiruvananthapuram. And each of them was a signature project on its own. The latest one Choice Marina, completed only in 2020, is an upmarket apartment complex with super spacious flats with the signature glass façade, specific to high-rise buildings in the Middle-east. Marina would soon become the favoured residential destination for the celebrities of Kerala.

'I have always taken immense pride in saying that I have played by the rulebook in all my deals. It was proving to be a difficult exercise to run the construction vertical purely on white money, which we somehow managed. Getting civic approvals and tackling bureaucratic red tape, many of them for no rhyme or reason, has been and continues to be cumbersome,' he says, acknowledging that the influx of fly-by-night builders spoiled the market by luring home-buyers with low rates for poorly built structures.

Squeezed between corrupt government officials perhaps not releasing files in anticipation of bribes and builders short-changing the customers on deliverables, Jose was forced to take a call on this vertical. Jose eventually decided to put the construction portfolio on the back burner.

Jose has never tried to hide his respect for Donald Trump as a developer, trying to build the best of facilities. His style and class have been an inspiration. Even as he justifies the decision for Choice to exit construction, the realty sector pundits point their finger at two defining factors. They say Choice construction catered mostly to the creamy layer, targeting the rich and the super-rich, at the best of times a niche market with limited volume.

Perhaps, Choice never became an entrenched player in the real estate market by gobbling up huge tracts of land and their sharp appreciation accounting for a significant share of profits for the company.

One thing is a given—Kerala, especially its business capital Kochi, will always treasure some of the landmark residential complexes built by Choice. One sure-fire way of assessing the worth of the many Choice residential units is the price they would fetch in the current market.

For Jose, this had but one purpose to serve, that of covering the gaping wound left by the millions he kept losing while chasing the elusive goal of owning a shipping line. Therefore, while he kept his Indian end going with construction as a new revenue source, back in the US, he kept pursuing any leads that came his way which would earn him a re-entry into shipping.

The year was 1991. It was the beginning of a new decade, and at the same time the countdown to the millennium had begun. It hurt him no end that all his initiatives to become ensconced in the shipping sector were being shattered. He was like a gambler, ready to roll the dice again, hoping to stem his losing streak in the high seas.

'Shipping had entered my bloodstream like an intoxicant. I was ready to do anything to realize my goal. That was just around the time when an Iraqi national called Dr Salman—the US head of operations, Thames Shipping Line, floated jointly by UAE, Qatar, Iran, Iraq and Kuwait—decided to start his own shipping line based out of London,' Jose discloses with a deep sigh.

There is a little known story, which Jose even now relives with a shudder about how he lost millions! Such was his obsession with becoming a big player in shipping that he went ahead and rented out an office in the World Trade Centre, which he is quick to add he used for both his shipping and seafood trade.

'When I heard Dr Salman was looking for an agent for the entire Indian subcontinent, there was no stopping me. It was only after I had invested millions of dollars into this venture that I heard the company was in trouble as a couple of ships were stuck in the Suez Canal. I was promised a partnership—a pan-India presence—so did not wish to believe this damning news. Dr Salman kept assuring me everything was okay, that it was only a temporary setback. Imagine my shock when just after a month, Thames Shipping Line shut down! Dr Salman vanished and my many millions evaporated,' he adds.

When he felt that everything was going as per plan, these headwinds hit the operations leading to financial instability. Jose would have to wait till 1995 to get a toehold once again in shipping. Fortunately, his shipping division—Choice Intermodal Services—would sign up as the south Indian agent of South Korean shipping major HMM (earlier Hyundai Merchant Marine), the same year that his airlines dream suffered a body blow.

14

THE SHRIMP KING

A BIG ADVANTAGE JOSE ENJOYED OVER MANY OF HIS PEERS back home was the toehold he managed to get in the US. This exposed him to two divergent economies, one ahead of the other by a few decades. Naturally, the advantage that he gained and one that he leveraged to the hilt was to go in for the transfer of technologies and ideas from the US to India.

The bold decision that changed the fundamentals of the way Choice engaged in seafood trade was his conviction that individual quick freezing (IQF) technology could be taken to India thus triggering a revolution in marine exports. So, there was that inevitable American connection behind Jose getting anointed the father of IQF technology in India.

The main end-users of shrimp from India were from Boston and Florida, where major factories thawed and cooked the products. The Brilliant Seafood Company in Boston used to buy the product, having mastered the IQF technology.

In Florida, he started befriending Tampa Singleton Seafood owned by Conagra Seafood which was arguably among the largest companies in the world. It was a smart play to offer his hand of friendship to the largest seafood company. Jose soon struck up a rapport with Jessy Gonsalvez who was the Singleton president. The Tampa engagement turned out to be a runaway success.

Soon, he began convincing others why they should join hands with him. He began persuading the global seafood giant Singleton to set up a plant in Kochi for manufacturing the final product in IQF form. An expert team was sent to Kochi. Their report showed that the cost of capital expenditure would be rewarded many times over by the overall cost saving on account of streamlining of the process and of course far more economical labour, thus making a competitively produced product that was processed at source.

It was agreed that Conagra would come up with 100 per cent capital expenditure and Singleton was to help Choice with technology support and buy back arrangements. On 26 September 1991, the first plant was inaugurated. All the seafood companies in Kerala were caught unawares.

Clearly, Jose was not satisfied for too long as a supplier only to the IQF plant in Florida. He wanted to replicate the Singleton model and found another large player to set up a plant under similar terms. By then, Jose had become an expert at erecting the IQF plant. At this stage, he was excited about adding one more customer. And it worked. The second IQF plant was established. Jose claims that he was the first person to set up a fully automated IQF plant to produce value-added products in India in association with his American technology partners.

The next six months witnessed a massive growth in business volumes for Choice and it kept that edge for eighteen to twenty-four months before others began catching up.

Though never acknowledged, Jose was the spark that led to the incursion of IQF technology into India.

The period between 1991 and 1994 was an economically stable period for the Choice Group. By 1993, with the onset of the new plant in Kochi, many companies perished, both in India and the US. Brilliant Seafood Company, that used to buy the best products from around the world and was acknowledged as the master of the IQF technology, was felled by Jose who was even at that time testing the waters for a US foray. John and Jim Randazzo, the owners of Brilliant Seafood, were forced to join Choice.

Mohan Varma, who was joint managing director of Choice till 1997, says Jose could make the IQF technology leap as he was always ready to go that extra mile. 'It is this mindset that led Jose to get into the IQF space which was hitherto sole domain of Japanese companies. Until then, it had been solely their privilege to import raw shrimp from India and then re-export it to the US and Europe after IQF treatment. Jose declared that he would have none of that.'

Jose targeted another high-profit area by getting into large volume black tiger shrimp cultivation using aqua culture. He set up a plant in Nellore exclusively for this purpose where he introduced cooking lines, he adds.

'It was entirely his initiative that brought Conagra to India and he put up the country's first IQF plant in Kochi in September 1991. I still remember how he went about purchasing the land where the plant was then located, from his mentor, Vikram Dholakia, a spices trader. This deal could take place only because Dholakia allowed a two-year window for the payment. Till Choice Group started the IQF plant, seafood was not profitable for the group,' points out Varma.

The next two years of unchallenged monopoly translated into never-before profits. Every week about three containers would get shipped out of Kochi, each with a value of ₹1.7 million. The rest of the marine exporters were still stuck with Block Frozen, whereas Choice had the clear edge, with many others struggling to keep pace with them.

'As the shipping agent of Ceylon Shipping Corporation, we had access to a dedicated feeder vessel, Lanka Muditha, that boasted of a minimal twenty-four hour delivery time to the international transhipment port at Colombo. That meant we were the only shipping agency in Kochi offering a weekly global window to local exporters via Colombo. No surprise for us that Jose was already planning his next move, a new production centre in Nellore, Andhra,' points out Varma.

Those were the days when Jose was fully immersed in the world of shipping as seafood was the least of his priorities. The truth is, the seafood sector offered nothing in comparison to the sense of adventure that was offered by the world of shipping.

His involvement in seafood exports, once the mainstay of the Choice Group, was mostly limited to the three months called kettu season for kara chemmeen or black tiger shrimp. He considered it a smelly business that was run mostly by uncouth proprietors and middlemen not averse to crude behaviour and language. Fortunately for Choice, that would change as Jose began infusing technology, hygiene and a modern work culture.

Subsequently, as others got into building IQF plants, fierce competition ensued. Many other American companies supported various newcomers in the IQF segment and profitability of Choice started to dwindle. Again, Jose was faced with the prospects of a failing business model.

'Jose always used to talk about his pet dream of starting Choice Shipping Lines. So, he tried like no other person would have, first with Maldives Shipping, followed by Ceylon Shipping, then US Lines and then the misadventure with Thames Shipping. Finally, when he got Hyundai Merchant Marine (HMM), he was happy to retain the position as their agent in south India. This was bound to happen as he had burnt his fingers far too many times while chasing big ticket dreams,' points out Varma.

Outright profits were scarce till the IQF advantage ensured a surge in cash flow and thus enhanced liquidity for Choice. However, these profits rarely resulted in a surge in liquidity for the Group. That was because Jose would almost always divert surplus funds to his many other ventures which more often than not were perpetually cash-strapped.

This was perhaps the reason why in the late '80s and early '90s, Choice Group entered greenfield projects as varied as residential buildings and education. As some of his former colleagues point out, Jose could not help himself from propping up ventures with money he could ill afford to divert from his core sector, which always was and should have remained the seafood industry.

The Backdrop

In the late '70s, the Kerala seafood industry was dominated by Kochi-based exporters, barring the odd ones based out of Chennai and Kozhikode. Among the main players were Amalgam Foods that added meat to its portfolio, Abad Fisheries, Chemmeens, Baby Marine, Choice Canning, Geo Seafood, Southern Seafoods, National Seafoods Company, Indo Marine Agency and India Seafood.

Some have downed shutters after years of struggle while others continue to thrive, having adapted themselves to emerging industry realities.

Says Shoukat Ali, managing partner of Kairali Exports, Ambalapuzha, who has been a keen follower of Jose for the past four decades, though they have never engaged in any business transactions:

'My interactions with Jose Sir date back to the late '70s, after I became a managing committee member of Seafood Exporters Association of India. When I joined the association, Chemmeens Cherian was the president. It was later that Sir took over as president. Those were the days when the entire industry was hit by the state government's decision to levy a hefty amount for the newly introduced Kerala Fishermen Welfare Fund. I started accompanying him to meet Chief Minister E.K. Nayanar, sometimes in his office but often at his official residence, Cliff House,' says Shoukat.

Shoukat recalls that Jose was assessed by the industry to be influential with central Cabinet ministers and the seafood industry was well aware of that. He remembers an occasion when the then Union Industries minister, P. Chidambaram, was the chief guest at a special meeting convened by the Marine Product Export Development Authority in Kochi. Shoukat says the Kerala seafood exporters will never forget when Chidambaram cut short his keynote address saying, 'I have a dinner appointment with Jose Thomas. Therefore, I must take leave of all of you now'.

The Kerala seafood export industry has witnessed alternating cycles of ups and downs, each lasting up to seven years. Let alone the marginal players, even the big seafood exporters usually see their fortunes take a dip during these lean periods. The present negative cycle began in 2018 and is expected to continue till about 2025. Curiously, Jose has seen his fortunes rise like never before ever since the pandemic hit the industry. But his peers are not sure whether this is yet another show of bravado.

'It is difficult to tell with Jose Sir. I have seen him during his good times and the bad phases, which I would come to know from others. And he used to smile all the time reassuring me that it is all part of the game, and I should not worry, as if it was my problem, and ask me to pray for him. Invariably, in the next meeting, he would pat my shoulder and say my prayers were useful, the troubles were over. As if I knew he had gone through a bad time,' concludes Shoukat.

The grooming lessons acquired during his US Lines days have played their part in creating a larger-than-life image of Jose. It was as if he realized pretty early in life the wisdom in projecting an enigmatic image about himself, a carefully crafted one that would not allow too many people to get close to him.

Clearly, his personality had begun evolving, as had his search for his true purpose in life. His mind was turbulent, struggling to figure out what he would do to make a sustained living, where he would live. It took him many more years and quite a few adventures before he found his true calling.

15

BLACK GOLD

THERE ARE MANY WHO FEEL JOSE WAS OFTEN GUILTY OF getting carried away the moment he sniffed a new opportunity, and poured in money without due diligence. That may be one way of looking at things, but why would the banks rush in with funds each time he came up with ambitious projects? Not many of JT's investment proposals were known to have been rejected by financial institutions. On the contrary, quite a few of them have vied with each other to bankroll his projects.

'He would suddenly spring a new investment plan on us. Not really a "plan" because we would get to know only after an asset acquisition involving a few million dollars. Then the ball would be tossed into the court of the finance department to raise the funds by stretching out payments to existing creditors or vendors. He would then approach banks or financial institutions when the deal was almost done, like a fait accompli,' elaborates Varma.

Consequently, the project funding in most cases used to happen after assets and resultant liabilities were created, often ignoring insufficient reserves. One must not forget that Choice went for these expansion projects in the seafood sector at a time when US Lines had crashed, Ceylon Shipping withdrew on account of privatization and Thames Shipping sucked out millions of dollars from the company coffers.

By then, he had started remodelling his seafood business with aquaculture or blue revolution as its centrepiece. Nellore became his centre of activity. It was in this region that shrimp could be grown artificially on land by pumping seawater into ponds.

It also entailed producing larvae in hatcheries, feeding and raising them, and after about 120 days, they would be ready for harvest. A new world of aquaculture opened up along the coastal belt of Andhra Pradesh, right from Nellore up to the border of Orissa. It was the sunrise industry of that time where young technicians were welcomed and supported by the landlords of Andhra. It was Jose's vision alone that made Choice embark on that journey, sacrificing the comfortable life of not only Kochi but also the luxury and excitement of living in New York.

Once again, the opportunity was seized by Jose who decided to get a toehold in the space hitherto occupied solely by the Japanese seafood industry. It was they who consumed huge volumes of the block-frozen black tiger shrimp in the raw form and further processing was done in their local factories. The numbers tell the story.

As against the normal shrimp exported from Kochi at ₹100 per kg, the tiger prawns had begun to fetch a price as high as ₹1,000 per kg. Till the time the black tiger prawn revolution began taking root in India in 1992–93, the well-established suppliers to the global market were Taiwan, Indonesia, and China. India was far away from the vicinity then.

Convincing the lead importer in Los Angeles to bypass the established suppliers and try out a newbie from India took some doing. Yet, Jose knew he was onto something akin to a gold rush and simply had to get on the gravy train. The unassailable part of the deal was that black tiger shrimp could be grown and harvested in such a manner that the product would be available round the year.

For once, India was ready to lead the Asian sea produce and emerge as the leading global supplier. The passion with which Jose pursued the Nellore dream is best captured by his wife, Elizabeth, who recalls the days that laid the foundation for the Choice Group resurgence.

'My twins were born, one month prematurely on the same day as the Nellore factory inauguration was scheduled. It was P. Chidambaram who inaugurated the factory and it was he who announced the happy news during his inaugural address. We used to travel by train, the whole family, ahead of the commissioning of the factory. We rented out a house in Nellore, one which we kept for almost four years, from 1991 to 1994,' says Elizabeth.

In value terms, the scope thrown up by black tiger shrimp was enormous as one container would fetch ₹90 lakh to ₹1 crore against ₹17 lakh that was the maximum return from one container of IQF shrimp. With John Z. Blazevich and his brand Contessa becoming involved in the Nellore operation, there was a sea change in the way the Choice plant was run, with focus on cleanliness, hygiene, dress code and quality control, unlike other processing plants along the Andhra–Orissa coast.

However, these profits were notional as Contessa had built in a process that would deduct many variables before arriving at the net payable amount.

'The system that Contessa put in place involved advancing a bulk amount, almost 80 per cent of the container cost and then chipping away from the amount in the name of those variables. Apart from the interest or capital servicing cost, there would be opportunity costs that would factor in the day of the product landing in the US and reducing a certain percentage for each day's delay. Eventually, the book profits would evaporate,' says Varma.

However, Jose was not bothered by these fine print details since he had long-term plans on his radar. First, there were the cooking lines for both Kochi and Nellore factories. It was decided to chisel out a piece of action from the Japanese by way of IQF facilities in India and so Choice began cutting into the Taiwanese and Chinese domination of black tiger shrimp.

The property for the Kochi IQF factory was acquired from veteran spice merchant Vikram Dholakia, who was also Jose's former mentor, on a deferred payment plan. It is only recently that the factory gave way to one of the most modern and pricey apartment projects in Kerala—Choice Marina. The Nellore property, too, was acquired from a local landlord, with a two-year grace period for completing the payment.

'Jose used to call black tiger shrimp "gold" and he stayed on and off in Nellore for two years to get the factory up and running. He turned the perception of the seafood trade on its head by bringing in a glamour quotient into the equation. There sixteen to twenty shrimps per pound (450 gm) pack but the number would decrease to eight to twelve as the size increased. The packs with lesser numbers would fetch a higher rate. So, he used to tell the women workers that each shrimp dropped meant a loss of ₹100. He used to personally mingle with the staff to usher in a sense of ownership among them,' adds Varma.

Unfortunately, neither the Nellore black tiger shrimp nor the IQF technology backed up with cooking lines could sustain the margins and so the losses began to mount. That was the time when most Asian currencies lost value and global trade went into a tailspin. The Nellore plant was no exception—it began to stagnate. The aquaculture farmers, the primary source of the shrimp, could not be paid, the factory started becoming inactive and the financial burden started ballooning.

The much-feted Nellore venture was by then bleeding. Things turned from bad to worse when Contessa, the main client for the processed black tiger shrimp, rejected a fresh consignment, citing quality issues.

The immediate fallout came as a body blow to Choice as it had to return $1 million to Contessa, having been paid for the consignment in advance. The damage went beyond $1 million as the rejection meant a possible blacklisting for Choice in the US market. Against all odds, Jose did a Houdini's act and turned things around as only he could. As is his wont, when one of his enterprises hits a downward spiral, he lets it be and turns his focus on a new venture.

The stage was set for him to get into the untested waters of construction and education. Over the next couple of decades, the school started by someone without any formal college education would emerge as the most coveted in the entire state. Though Jose would build some of the most iconic high-rise residential buildings in Kochi, his claim to fame would come from his school—a venture many of his peers questioned, coming from a man whose education never went beyond class 11, in those days called pre-degree.

Cutting across all these forays, at the same time binding them together, was the innate strength he acquired in what was finally emerging as his core activity. For a young man, who was made fun of by his relatives in old Madras with the nickname, Chemmeen Jose, it was quite the case of poetic justice when he began getting acknowledged by many of his associates in the US as 'Shrimp King'.

But his one peeve that sometimes raises its head is that he never got due credit at home for the pioneering role he played in bringing IQF technology to India. Being called Shrimp King by his associates in the US is one thing but getting feted with a sobriquet 'father of IQF tech in India' would have been something else. Alas! That was not to be.

16

NO BRICK ON THE WALL

IN THE EARLY SIXTIES, THERE WAS A STORY DOING THE rounds in the textile city, Ahmedabad, about why the noted physicist and father of Indian space technology, Vikram Sarabhai, had begun to set up the Indian Institute of Management, Ahmedabad (IIMA), in 1961. It was said in light banter that perhaps Sarabhai wanted his mercurial daughter, Mallika Sarabhai, not to leave home for her higher studies.

Quite a far-fetched tale, as stories go, because IIMA was started in December 1961 with Ravi Mathai as the founding director. Though Mallika did join IIMA, it was much later, in 1972.

For Jose, who had returned from the US and was actively looking out for good schools for his first two children, the available fare was far from what he could describe as desirable. The classrooms were like matchboxes; there was meagre ventilation, no fans to keep the children comfortable in the tropical heat. Add to that the pathetic excuses that went by in the name of bathrooms, the smelly urinals that were the order of the day, and the dismal picture was complete.

Thus, having diversified into the construction sector that required interaction with the public, for Jose, it was a toss-up between starting a hospital or a school. There was much debate in the family and among the top managers about the pros and cons of both. Finally, Jose decided it had to be a school, but one that was completely different from what was on offer around them.

In 1990, Jose, who was in his mid-thirties had begun mulling over the necessity of creating a legacy. As the Choice Group was thinking in terms of CSR and brand building, it was natural that both these goals dovetailed into a single mission.

'I thought it best to throw the question open to some of the big names in the city so that they would ratify my decision to set up a school. We convened a townhall with a few hundred influential people, many of them potential parents in attendance. I remember there were four of us on the dais and the other three started speaking one after the other. I was very nervous, and actually started dreading the moment I would have to make the keynote speech,' Jose travels back in time to that critical day that would go on to define his legacy.

Then came an unexpected intervention, while the principal designate was speaking—Jose was handed over an anonymous note by one of his associates from the backstage area who said it came from someone in the audience. He read the note: 'You have not even completed your pre-degree. Are you qualified to run a school?'

That got Jose's adrenaline going. It was a challenge thrown and readily accepted. Unknown to the one who scribbled the note, he weighed in albeit inadvertently as the one who forced Jose's hand.

'I decided then and there that I would leave no stone unturned to establish the best school in the city, maybe even in the state,' says Jose, who believes that the note was the singular factor that clinched the decision for Choice to get into education.

Choice took over the South Point School in the upmarket Panampilly Nagar. There were ninety-seven students and the parents were told they had the option to take their wards out. Providentially, none did. The Choice School officially started functioning on 26 June 1991. At the helm was the principal, supported by six teachers. The overriding ideology was that the school would be child-centric for a change and not one that revolved around teachers.

Jose was like a man possessed. He purchased fourteen acres in Tripunithura within a year, built an entire block to accommodate between 500 to 1,000 students and shifted out in 1993 when a boarding facility was also added to absorb NRI students and those hailing from families of rubber planters and NRIs from pockets in Kottayam like Kanjirapally and even the Malabar region.

In 1998, the first batch of grade 10 students passed out from Choice School and the first crop of grade 12 in 2000, by which time Choice School, Tripunithura, was `the school' to attend in Kerala. The number of students started swelling, which in turn meant more divisions and more teachers as Jose refused to allow more than twenty-five students in one class. In just over ten years, Choice School had 2,000 students!

As Choice School approached its silver jubilee year, the debate began on the need to become a multi-location education venture. The Thiruvalla school is a hub connecting the residential spokes of Changanassery, Kottayam, Alappuzha and Kozhencherry.

The foundation stone was laid in January 2015 and the school started functioning with 100 students in June 2015.

The 45,000 square feet school complex, was completed in the third quarter of 2019, spread over 8 acres has already won six international awards for its architectural excellence.

The Choice School, Thiruvalla, turned out its first batch of grade 10 students in 2022. The Choice School, Kozhikode, spread over 11 acres and located in the vicinity of a medical college and an engineering college, will come of age in 2025 with grade 10 pass-outs. Between the three locations, Jose in his role as educator, would be guiding around 4,000 students.

Despite the massive disruptions brought about in the field of education by the pandemic, the USP of Choice Schools remains uninterrupted. It is the mantra of student-centred education, with teachers acting as facilitators or mentors. The crux of the vision is that the teachers no longer treat students as mere bricks on the wall, cogs in the otherwise faceless education machinery.

Even as he basks under the sunshine of his very successful US seafood enterprise and an Indian side that is finally showing signs of settling down, Jose takes more pride in what he has achieved with his schools. And certainly not without reason. It is Choice School that has earned him a name in society—much more than being a businessman with factories in India and the US. Similarly, not many people know him as a shipping agent who associated in such a big way with major shipping lines despite all the time and effort he put in there. Nor is it any different for him as the builder of many iconic buildings in his city.

In a nutshell, Jose is more popular as the man who set up Choice School than for his many other pursuits in life. And that also happens to yield him more return on investments than all other verticals put together.

17

BECOMING JT

IT IS AN UNDISPUTED TRUTH THAT JOSE WAS NEVER SATISFIED being confined to the role of the unassuming seafood exporter. Nor was he ready to live out his days as a shipping associate. He would happily accept all his setbacks for getting a chance to play the Samurai of the seven seas who made his fortune by rescuing and delivering cargo from stranded vessels to the pirate-infested Sudan coast.

Once a shy boy from Fort Kochi, Jose's transformation was phenomenal when he started hobnobbing with the political brass in Sri Lanka, when he received the US project on a platter. Since the next two years witnessed a significant boom in the company's fortunes as the only-player-in-India status of the Choice IQF, these developments prompted him to create a new persona for himself befitting his achievements.

The first visible impact of the IQF success story was the image makeover that Jose Thomas decided to undertake by way of creating a corporate headquarters for his growing business activities. The need was genuine as what was till then a seafood export company had grown to add outstanding shipping activities to its portfolio, with the likes of Ceylon Shipping and US Lines in its client list.

The Choice Group had also started making considerable strides in construction. Parallel to the brand-building initiatives, Choice School was beginning to make waves. Add to all that the US connection and Jose suddenly had a full platter to offer and befitting corporate headquarters could no longer be denied.

Jose realized that if Choice Trading were to evolve into a big business group with interests spanning two continents, it needed a new corporate identity. He signalled his decision to move out of the Willington Island office located in Ninan's Cold Storage building.

The initial plan was to occupy one floor of a three-storey building in Atlantis, right opposite Cochin Shipyard. It was also symbolic in the sense that Choice was getting a makeover—from being an old Cochin company to one that would now be housed in the new city. Somehow, the one-floor plan gave way to Jose's decision to occupy the entire building.

Jose astonished everyone by leasing out the entire building, almost 25,000 square feet, including a massive terrace. By the time the office was furnished, the bill came to about ₹1.5 million.

But all this would not have meant much until he suddenly went for an image makeover exercise. In a world where brands sell products, he decided there was nothing untoward in rebranding himself. It was towards mid-1992 that Jose started getting addressed as JT, essentially the initials of his name. And he knew he was on to a good thing.

'I think it was one of my nephews who first started calling me JT, maybe as he felt calling me uncle or Jose Achayan was not professional. And I have, over the years, got more comfortable being addressed by my initials,' says Jose.

It could not have happened at a more opportune time as Choice was leading the rest of the seafood exporting houses in the country on a merry dance, thanks to its new operating partner, Conagra.

By then, most in the top management team had got used to the expansive ways of their boss. They knew he could suddenly push the pedal and start scaling up operations based on his instinct, rather than being dictated by sound business numbers.

Invariably, it was the finance department that was left with the onerous task of finding ways to cover the latest bill. Many saw it as wasteful expenditure, an unnecessary splurge by a newbie entrepreneur flush with funds. However, for JT, nothing was wasteful as even the most lavish of spends would more often than not lead to a high return on investment at the least expected juncture.

'It was not out of character as not many in India would have known that around the same period JT acquired his first US office, at 19, Rector Street, Manhattan, New York. Soon, he would also go on to acquire an office on behalf of Ceylon Shipping, but one totally under his control. Well, it was nowhere else but in the coveted World Trade Center. I was taken aback because during my early visits to the US, he would take me around and always stop in front of the World Trade Center and say he would one day have an office there and I would laugh it off as his fantasy. Yet, JT found a way to turn this fantasy into reality,' recollects Varma.

Though JT has never held back from celebrating life, it is no secret that he would do so only the way he saw fit, and only with people he felt comfortable with. In that sense, he was never one to be seen in public functions unless they were curated by him, that too with a specific purpose in mind. Therefore, when he felt the time was ripe for the people in Kochi to see him as someone at ease with celebrities, he chose to host a community that anyone could relate to with ease—the best cricketers of India.

Thus, it was after much planning that JT hosted a friendly match between Kapil Dev's XI and Sunil Gavaskar's XI in Kochi. The occasion showcased Sachin Tendulkar in his early teens as well as veteran cricketers including Syed Kirmani, Krishnamachari Srikkanth, Ajit Wadekar and Ravi Shastri.

One man who continued to be a part of his inner circle and who had also played a lifesaving innings for him was Kapil Dev. As discussed earlier, if it were not for Kapil's timely intervention, JT's major foray into construction would have floundered at the very beginning.

Meanwhile, it was perhaps this opportunity to rub shoulders with the people who mattered to a young and vibrant India, on the threshold of economic liberalization, that infused JT with the confidence to aim for the sky. JT started cultivating the friendship of political leaders like P. Chidambaram, Subramanian Swamy, K. Karunakaran and Ghulam Nabi Azad.

This confidence rubbed off on the US operations of Choice as it happened around the time John and Jim Randazzo of Brilliant Seafood Company joined JT. For him, it was always about getting good people on board, those who could share his vision. Avis Viswanathan, who first met Jose Thomas in 1991 for a story that he was writing for a national magazine on the booming seafood exports industry, shares how JT transformed his life.

'In December 1991, he told me that he was planning a two-week trip to Japan and wanted me to come along. Let me show you the world. I remember asking him, in return for what? And he shot back saying that I just want to show you the world. In February 1992, I joined him in Tokyo as his guest on a two-week tour. One evening, over a traditional Japanese meal, he made me an offer to join Choice Group,' says Avis.

Avis worked with JT for only a year but that was at a critical juncture when Jose was metamorphosing into a brand. Yes, JT began propagating the brand through himself. He was not just the brand ambassador but the brand itself, one that he wanted to take beyond the confines of south India and a certain part of the US.

'He believed in people. He always wanted people to do well. So, he gave them opportunities, taught them skills, helped them see the world differently—full of possibilities. A world where business is transacted, a world where people who worked hard and had imagination could succeed. His ideas were way ahead of his time.'

JT often admits it was always his dream to start the Choice Shipping Lines. Yet, it was not a shipping company but an airlines company that he went all out for, with absolutely no background in the aviation sector. JT had made up his mind that it was now or never for him as he pounced on the unlikeliest of opportunities to reposition his hitherto little-known Choice in the transnational arena.

It was a decision that confounded many. In later days, debates would rage as to why JT would gamble it all away, because going for broke to enter the rarefied field of aviation was nothing short of a gamble. In retrospect, there is only one way to explain this flutter by JT. It was as if he was possessed by a spirit!

That spirit was none other than that of young Jose, who for some time had been tucked away under the recesses of the painstakingly constructed persona of JT. Lurking in the periphery but always ready to come out was Jose, shorn of all shackles, free to express himself in a world where even angels feared to tread!

18

EYE IN THE SKY

THIS IS A STORY ABOUT HOW BIG JT WAS WILLING TO GO with his ideas, irrespective of whether they stood a realistic chance to succeed or not. His calling, as he saw it, was to aim for the sky—and in this case, literally so!

Some of his efforts took wings, others crash-landed. A few of those that failed did so spectacularly. The capers that he did pull off in the most unlikely manner were breathtaking and yet, the ventures that famously floundered would have been even more spectacular had he succeeded.

Many of his forays were in sectors allied to his core activities, though some were in the most unexpected verticals. Curiously, a number of his initiatives in his core segments faced reverses whereas a handful of his forays in totally untested waters turned into roaring success stories.

There was one big quantum leap he attempted, moving away from his comfort zone on the high seas to aim to fly the Indian skies. The many factors that went into the making of the story of that one singularly ambitious venture makes one pose the question—did JT really believe he could have pulled it off?

This dark episode has been described by industry pundits variously as JT attempting to punch above his weight and his flight of fantasy. He, however, believes it was no fantasy, that he did make the right moves. He had nearly pulled it off when Choice Airlines came crashing down and with it, the entire Choice Group. Well, almost!

The period was 1993–94. Just over a year had passed after India was bitten by the liberalization bug. P.V. Narasimha Rao was prime minister and Manmohan Singh, the country's finance minister. There was a buzz in the air, as India was poised to integrate with the world economy.

Debates raged over comparative benefits of the private sector taking control over critical sectors, whether it had the ability to take the baton, to run the long race. The Soviet terminologies, Glasnost and Perestroika, were freely being interspersed while analysing the opening up of the Indian economy.

One natural corollary was India's strategic decision to open up its skies to private airline companies. So, what was JT doing there? Sure, he had been taking flying lessons but he was nowhere close to landing his commercial flying licence. Therefore, it would be misleading to assume that he decided to start an airline company so as to start knocking on the doors of the pilots' club.

The fact of the matter was, JT was flush with funds—at least on paper. His new company, Choice Canning Inc, was fast getting established in the US. Back home, the two new ventures, Choice Construction and the food-processing business, were faring remarkably well. He had managed an image makeover for his seafood business by starting a new facility near Nellore in Andhra Pradesh. As it is with any new project, the Nellore project was bleeding money.

He still nurtured big hopes of emerging as a major player in shipping, a few setbacks notwithstanding. Hyundai Merchant Marine and JT were like to two peas in a pod. He had set up a corporate office back home in Cochin that many of his peers could only dream of. Above all this, probably after a long period, he was enjoying the kind of liquidity he had rarely witnessed before. But the harsh reality, perhaps something known only to his finance department, was that they were borrowing from Peter to pay Paul.

To this day, JT fiercely defends his decision to foray into something as unrelated as commercial airlines. He is steadfast in his claim that he reached this decision on merit. It was simply in keeping with his usual style—he saw a great opportunity and went all out for it.

In that sense, there really was nothing out of place in trying to master the Indian skies. His basic nature has always been to seize a good opportunity by the scruff of the neck. In this instance, he saw an immense opportunity.

However, there are quite a few who believe that he was led up the garden path by some of his trusted lieutenants in that period. Those who have followed JT's track record should not have been surprised when he threw his hat in the ring to turn 'air taxi operator' of the Indian skies. The reality, however, is that everyone was taken aback.

The decision regarding a huge diversification that meant an entry into the green field aviation sector came as a big surprise also for senior company managers as Choice Group was facing considerable cash flow issues. There were national media reports about the world's second-largest shipping line with air operations hitherto limited to only the Scandinavian region getting ready to test the Indian skies. There were also reports about an unnamed Kochi-based company being in talks with Maersk for the airline project. Only those who knew JT from his early days may have realized that the big-ticket move to capture the skies was one big gamble to set things right with his core activity—seafood business.

That would come later. It all began when JT was tipped off that Maersk Shipping's airline division was looking to expand beyond its limited Scandinavian footprint. Given India's global positioning in the post-economic liberalization period, there was some chatter in the international aviation circles about India being on their radar.

One of his erstwhile contacts from Maersk Shipping, whom he met in Singapore, tipped him off: it could be a potential opportunity for him. On the face of it, there should be no connection between JT's exposure to Ceylon Shipping, his increased access to the Sri Lankan political establishment, his bid along with Maersk Marine Software for the Nhava Sheva port operator licence and joining up as a consortium partner with Maersk Air to bid for Indian air taxi licence in 1994.

Yet, it was evident that there was an underlying connection between these seemingly random variables. Simply put, JT thought he could forge a whole new metal from the melting pot that was his past associations.

It is now history that Maersk would mark the beginning of a wide network as the port operator in 2004 when A.P. Moeller Terminals, which later came to be known as Gateway Terminals India, became the operator of Nhava Sheva Port in Navi Mumbai. 'Though not known to many, why, it is not even there in the Choice archives, it was the Choice Group that got Maersk to consider a project in India,' says JT.

'The year was 1992 and we managed to get a technical division of Maersk Shipping to make a joint bid with Choice for the position of the Nhava Sheva port operator. That was not to be, but I continued engaging with them, visiting their facilities in Copenhagen. Eventually, my persistence paid off when I convinced the airlines division of Maersk to join us as the consortium partner while bidding for the coveted air taxi licence in India.'

'I had reason to believe I stood a fair chance of clinching an air taxi licence as per the terms stipulated by the Indian government. It required me to take many trips to Copenhagen, numerous meetings with the operations head of Maersk Air, Capt. Gustavson, and eventually with the group chairman, A.P. Moeller. I had only one goal—to convince them that I was the right partner for them. Fortunately for me, they were already mulling an entry into India as they saw a long-term opportunity here,' says JT.

The level of confidence about pulling off the deal was so high that JT started hiring pilots back home, quite a few from the national domestic carrier, Indian Airlines. His Cochin office started wearing all the trappings of an airline company, the newly hired staff giving off the impression they were all part of a soon-to-be-launched airlines company, with its proposed headquarters in Chennai.

JT was busy tying up the loose ends in Denmark. In hindsight, he ought to have been concentrating more on getting things streamlined with the Indian Civil Aviation Ministry.

'They flew me in their Boeing 737 from Copenhagen to Billund in the cockpit along with the pilots and ran through the various steps of reducing the back-drag and as a result reducing excessive fuel burn. This made sense as fuel cost accounts for about 60 per cent of the airline expenditure,' says JT.

'The MoU was signed by Moeller and me; my wife was present on that momentous occasion and I was floating like a cloud in the sky. In my mind, I was already running the latest air taxi service in India,' he adds with a rueful smile, the hurt still visible on his face after so many years.

Then followed the grand MoU signing ceremony in Chennai, where the celebrations went on through the night. Within days, the Danes started landing in Kochi, Choice started compiling data on their behalf regarding trunk route traffic. The finance department was on tenterhooks, as the new scale of operations opened up worry lines about fund availability. True to form, JT told them not to worry because he never had the luxury of starting any new project with funds in hand, and this was no exception.

The plan was to keep the entire system ready to go. The list included seasoned pilots, trained stewardesses, efficient ground staff, the works. The Choice HQ in Kochi resembled a five-star hotel. Senior pilot, Jeff, along with his associates began camping in large numbers at Taj Malabar. They were scheduled for immediate hiring. A few even put in their papers at the national domestic carrier, Indian Airlines, betting on JT's new venture becoming a runaway success!

The due diligence by Maersk must surely have stumbled on the Choice Group's meagre cash reserves but they were bowled over by the 100-odd employees of Choice seafood vertical, all in uniform and sending out the correct corporate vibe. There were clearly hundreds of moneyed parents reposing complete faith in JT with the future of their children at stake.

The aura of trust that surrounded the Choice Group seemed impenetrable. Add to that the impressive track record associating with big shipping lines and a thriving construction wing that built fashionable homes. It was thus a full platter, difficult for the Maersk team to ignore.

'The icing on the cake of course was the mind-blowing corporate headquarters where the managing director stood in a queue at the cafeteria and the staff partied after work at the recreation facility. Then there was the impressive personality of JT who rubbed shoulders with the who's who of the Indian government. Maersk was convinced they had found the right partner,' says Varma.

There were two things happening side by side. The first was the setting up of a temporary operations base in Delhi so that JT could pursue the air taxi foray while in residence. Being the Indian partner of a consortium where the other party was the Denmark-headquartered Maersk Air, Choice was expected to do all the grassroots level facilitating with the politicians and the aviation department.

In those days, there were no project consultants who would manage the entire work on a turnkey basis. JT soon realized that the onus was on him to lobby for his air taxi licence. That meant only one thing in the India of those days. As he began networking with politicians in Delhi, his proximity to the former chief minister of Kerala came to his aid as he was then the Union Cabinet Minister for Industries. There was no dearth of MPs from his home state, most of whom began frequenting JT's makeshift headquarters in the centrally located Hotel Taj Palace in Chanakyapuri, home to scores of embassies and consulates. But his self-designated task, of befriending Civil Aviation Minister Ghulab Nabi Azad remained unfinished.

He was caught up in the excitement and the resultant adrenalin rush that is special to the capital of the country where you get to rub shoulders with India's decision-makers.

JT was flying high, with many of his associates treating him as if he was already the owner of a domestic airline. Money kept flowing in as no expenditure was deemed beyond limits. Lavish parties were thrown, as he went all out to gain a foothold in the Delhi social circuit.

During his prolonged stays in Delhi, he started interacting in a big way with self-declared power brokers such as Chandra Swamy, kingmakers like Vincent George, the personal assistant of Rajiv Gandhi. Subramanian Swamy also stepped in to support JT.

'We already had an office going in Chennai for Choice Air, about a dozen pilots were already on board, signed on at fancy salaries. The splurge rippled down to other Choice offices,' JT recalls with a sense of dread as to what followed once the bubble burst.

Capt. Jeff, who was in charge of the crew, played a major role in recruiting a number of fellow pilots from Indian Airlines. He recalls, 'That was a sad chapter in our lives. I remember as if it was yesterday, the image of Choice colours painted on six aircrafts belonging to Maersk Air. It was a stunning blow. Many of the pilots went back and some joined other airlines that had started operations by then. I joined Kingfisher Airlines as Chief Synthetic Flight Instructor in 2005,' reminisces Capt. Jeff.

Capt. Jeff, officially Geoffrey Jesudason, was director training, Indian Airlines, for almost four years when he took the plunge and joined hands with his friend of many years, JT. He flew officially for the last time when the national carrier honoured him with what was not unlike a lap of honour by asking him to take control in the cockpit.

At the age of sixty-five, he got his signing off flight, from Mumbai to Delhi, in 2012. Now, a good decade later, he wonders how fate conspired to make him miss out on what might easily have been the most challenging task in his career, as the head of operations at Choice Air.

The fact remains that Choice was a wildcard entry. The others in the fray were Jet Airways, led by the canny Naresh Goyal, and a few others. There was no doubt whatsoever even then that JT was punching considerably above his weight.

What also transpired simultaneously was the decision to take Choice Trading Corporation Pvt Ltd public by going in for an IPO. The plan was simple enough. He needed capital to give flight to his Choice Air project in proportion to Choice as the lead partner of the consortium with Maersk Air. The IPO managers were Kotak Mahindra, along with State Bank of India.

'I recall the many road shows that I went on with Uday Kotak, for whom this would have probably been among the initial lot of IPOs. Post valuation, the Choice Trading listing price was fixed at ₹60 per ₹10 share. The primary objective of the public issue being funding the Choice Air venture; there was a built-in clause that the IPO could take place subject to the company getting the air taxi licence from the Ministry of Civil Aviation. The moment the licence fell through, the IPO became null and void,' says JT with a shudder.

For one who has had his fair share of setbacks in life, those days were among the darkest JT has lived through. As the days grew into weeks and weeks into months, all JT remembers is the dark haze that clouded his mind. Any psychologist would say that was the inbuilt escape button provided by the human mind, because to relive that period day-by-day would drive any sane person up the wall.

Though the immediate loss to the company balance sheet was to the tune of ₹900 million, JT maintains the practical damage in today's terms was to the tune of ₹30 billion. This would be in terms of other activities of the group that were negatively impacted and fresh opportunities lost. The ripples from this debacle over a quarter-century ago still make its presence felt, admits JT with a rueful smile.

Says Varma, who had a ringside view of what transpired in those eventful days, 'JT was close to many in the corridors of power in Delhi. He had even signed on the services of a number of politicians to lobby for Choice Air for which payments were made, with proper receipts. I vividly remember one of them insisting on signing the receipt for his fee, with the assurance that an in-principle clean chit has been given by Prime Minister Narasimha Rao.'

It was the buzz then that the Queen of Denmark, who came on a visit to India, was understood to have underlined Maersk's interest in getting the air taxi licence. So, what went wrong? What really triggered the proverbial slip between the cup and the lip?

There was a theory, though unfounded, that it was East–West Airlines that prevailed upon Civil Aviation Minister Ghulam Nabi Azad not to allow Choice Air to get going as an air taxi operator. The reason cited was simple: in those days, the considerable traffic of non-resident Keralites, mostly from the GCC nations, both incoming and outgoing, was routed through Mumbai as there were no direct flights to Kerala. East–West Airlines, which was then servicing a good number of these passengers, saw Choice Air as a real threat.

Those in the know of the goings-on in Delhi those days feel that JT reposed too much trust and spent piles of money on people who were only bystanders to the real play in the Indian skies. If he had established a direct link with the aviation minister or the only one who could veto him, the Prime Minister, things may have turned out differently.

Those who engaged were only passing on information regarding what had already transpired and that too at the behest of the Danish company, like the Queen interceding on behalf of Maersk. They also say that the fact that Choice did not have any exposure in the airlines sector made it easy for Azad to reject its bid.

The fall-out had disastrous consequences for the Choice Group. JT had to pay a huge price for underestimating the deals that could be struck through back-route channels. All this, while he was making a grand but misguided effort to fashion a decision in his favour through the lobbyists and pressure groups.

In hindsight, he went wrong by reposing too much faith on having Maersk as his consortium partner but failing to cover his bets in the dangerous playground of deal-makers that was Delhi. Though only an MoU was signed between Choice and Maersk, it had been informally accepted that the airline venture would take many years to stabilize, incurring a loss of ₹400 million a year, which would continue till 2020 which was when an operational break-even was expected. As an equal equity partner, Choice would have to share this loss.

'Hence, it had been informally decided, Choice would settle for a marginal equity stake, as low as 5 per cent. However, the name of the company would be Choice Air; JT would be the president. Maersk was happy with this formula,' says Varma shedding light on the strategic decisions taken to ensure smooth sailing for the Indo–Denmark joint venture before the Civil Aviation Ministry pulled the plug on Choice Air.

JT was dealt a huge blow and the company suffered an enormous financial setback despite his remarkable ability to convert half chances into viable opportunities.

'I remember Dad used to have a Boeing aircraft poster with the Choice Air insignia on it hanging from the wall of his office cabin. Then, one day he tore it down. That is how

I knew our airline venture was not going to happen,' says his son, Thomas.

In retrospect, JT should have had his guard up against behind-the-scenes manoeuvrings by the established players to keep a newbie like the Choice Group out of the reckoning. Not even the good word put in by the Queen of Denmark for the Maersk entry into the Indian skies to the Indian Prime Minister could tilt the balance. The body blow proved more debilitating to Choice than to Maersk.

Does he regret having made a grab, albeit a failed one, for a pie in the Indian sky? JT firmly says no. 'It cannot be held against me if I set my aspirations high. It was not that I was daydreaming, I followed through on my instinct for what would have been a stunningly bold decision with considerable passion, by going all out for that licence. Sure, I made some big mistakes in the way I went about it. I would do it all over again, but differently,' JT rationalizes.

In the final analysis, one spur-of-the-moment decision, always the hallmark of the irrepressible Jose, had let down the Choice Group in a monumental way. It would take many years for JT to learn how to allow the adventure-seeking young Jose in him to make only restricted appearances.

The alternate reality, the one subscribed to by many who have been keeping a close tab on the goings-on at Choice Group is that Jose has managed to wear the persona of JT for longer periods of time, allowing his adventure-seeking true self to paint the big canvas only once in a blue moon. This lack of practice impaired his lobbying skills.

This endless jostling for mind space by these two personalities would have kept the likes of Sigmund Freud and Carl Jung feuding over their inference of the real deal.

19

IN FREE FALL

THE DAMAGE WREAKED BY THE FAILED AIR TAXI LICENCE bid to Choice Group's financial structure was perhaps not as long-lasting as the dent left on its corporate image. It was an even bigger setback for JT personally. By early 1995, rumours began flying thick and fast back home in Kochi that JT's empire was on the verge of collapse. He began facing enquiries from various quarters whether the group was in trouble.

His response was aggressive, even a bit antsy, as he conveyed the message that they better keep their distance: 'Yes, I am in big trouble. Why do you ask? Are you in a position to help, may be lend me some money?' Such in-your-face snubs resulted in two things—many of them stopped asking seemingly well-meaning, solicitous questions. The other unavoidable outcome was many of his peers started keeping a safe distance from him, no doubt fearing his sharp tongue.

'My real response was a big statement to all those who were waiting for my company to fold up. I put on the mother of all performances to declare to the world that my hand was not yet fully played. Where else could I do it but at the Taj Malabar, always my haven in times of trouble,' he says with a cheeky smile.

The act of bravado was not an easy one to pull off. On the one hand, considerable funds from the core activity of seafood exports got diverted into a venture that failed to take off. The overdrafts kept mounting, the company was leveraged beyond viability; neither could the debt be serviced nor the rising interest be paid.

He was caught in a classic debt trap. Having registered Choice Trading as a deemed public company, the company needed to declare its profit and loss account for the financial year, by reporting its balance sheet on March 31.

'The bankers and auditors were breathing down my neck. I had to reverse the downward slide by ensuring that the company's net worth did not stand eroded by the cascading debt. My auditors recommended that I file for bankruptcy under the BIFR norms. For me, that was an option worse than a death sentence. I grabbed at the only lifeline available, which was to avail the option to extend our financial year by 180 days, till September 30,' says JT with evident unease as he struggles with memories of those dark days.

It was only a temporary solution. Many thought he was only given a long rope; that he would fail to do anything with the time he had bought. As he started setting his house in order, what he could not reconcile himself with was ₹160 million on the liabilities side, which were outstanding dues to about fifty vendors.

'I needed at least ₹100 million as working capital to buy raw material, in this case, mostly shrimp. As my entire revenue chain was dependent on this, the banks were outright refusing any more loans. On the contrary, they were threatening to auction my assets, before I claimed bankruptcy. That is when the most unlikely man entered my life, though indirectly—Gautam Adani,' remembers JT. Gautam Adani, one of the richest men in the world now, who was at that point of time getting started as an exporter, turned out to be a lifeline for JT's business, who therefore was lucky to be associated with him even in a small way.

In those days, Adani Exports was frantically ramping up its export volumes to make the grade as a Star Export House to get various tax breaks as also other incentives from the DGFT (Director General of Foreign Trade). The company had sent out its representatives to various port cities and was offering a 10 per cent margin for generating fresh business opportunities.

JT recalls how he got to meet Gautambhai, as he is known at his Ahmedabad home. 'I vividly remember taking Adani's representative, Veeramani Swami, on my yacht—the Choice Queen—and persuading him to get me an appointment with Gautambhai. Soon, we flew up to Ahmedabad where I met him at his home. He gave me a patient hearing. I remember he even had a smile on his face when I finally made my pitch, as if he had anticipated something like this.'

Adani was non-committal, did not say much but promised he would intimate his decision soon. JT could only keep his fingers crossed as he returned home. It was a mixture of relief and elation that he felt when Veeramani called him a few days later to convey Adani's decision. He had agreed to JT's proposal which was nothing short of a bail-out plan!

'I breathed easy only after receiving faxed copies of drafts of ₹10 million, ₹15 million and so on, till the total amount that came into my account stood at ₹100 million. On reflection, my proposal to Gautambhai was quite outrageous as he was required to advance me the entire margin money of ₹100 million, so that I would line up exports worth ₹1 billion to Adani Exports,' JT opens up on what saved him from bankruptcy.

It was probably JT's disclosure on how he dared to compete for the Indian skies with the likes of Tatas and Jet Air that convinced Adani, who himself is celebrated for his capacity to take risks. Sure, a risk taker on a much smaller scale, but Gautam Adani who had had his share of rough patches to weather in his early days, could easily empathize with the plight of another entrepreneur taking bold decisions to get himself out of a tight corner.

Says Arvin Varghese, who would go on to become one of JT's trusted men in the US, before branching out on his own, 'Among other things, I was assigned very interesting odd jobs, like picking up Gautam Adani's representative Veeramani from the airport. I had to keep him entertained till JT took over playing host.'

'The other chore was to have me wait near the fax machine for the photocopy of the advance payment of ₹100 million from Adani. That was what kept the Choice Group afloat at that point of time. For one year, I also had the task of reassuring Azeez, a vendor in Nellore, that his outstanding ₹2 million was safe,' he adds.

Arvin's stint with JT had started when he was twenty-one, in 1996, barely a year after the Choice Air meltdown. The team then used to work through the night at Choice HQ in Atlantis. There were smartly dressed ladies who had been hired to train air hostesses still bustling around. Young Arvin used to wonder why they were still there as things were not good financially.

Arvin would come to know later that it was the group's policy not to fire anyone, by giving them enough landing time either to get absorbed by other divisions, or to find another job. What he saw then, as one who closely observed what was happening around him, was how other divisions of Choice like seafood, shipping, construction and education were hurting because of the airline foray.

The irony is that not many knew how devastated JT was soon after the days of the Choice Air collapse. Consequently, they were equally unaware of his recharged frame of mind after returning from Ahmedabad.

'I carried on with the late-night parties in Choice House, Kochi, thereby putting forth an image of someone with no care in the world. Those were the days when my vendors to whom I owed considerable money, would come into my office and abuse me. I did not show them how shaken I was, Therefore, when I called all my vendors, about four dozen of them, for a grand dinner at Taj Malabar and ploughed them with costly liquor, they did not know how to react,' JT recalls.

However, this mother of all dinners, at least in JT's life, deserves a more elaborate narration. JT decided to throw a lavish party at the iconic Malabar Hotel on the Island for his many creditors. He invited each and every one of his over four dozen sundry creditors, who he was in no position to pay off immediately if he was to keep his seafood exports going. It was a grand party, almost like a wedding reception and JT, the lavish host, not unlike a bridegroom's father.

They could see the sumptuous dinner ready to be served as the smell began wafting through the air. They could also see the pricey liquor bottles neatly arrayed at the makeshift bar counter. Above all, there was this magical spell of the location, arguably the most pricey hospitality destination in the state.

With this surreal snob factor working against them, the invitees did not know what hit them when JT came up with his deferred repayment plan. It was pretty much the slaughter of the lambs! One person who recalls what happened that night like yesterday is Suresh KPN, the Kochi head of Sundaram Finance. 'Nonchalantly, he asked his fifty-odd creditors to decide if they wanted their money or not. This was the gist of JT's speech as I remember it: "You all have two options. One, allow me to carry on. This will keep alive the chance of you being repaid, over a period of time. Or, you can stop my activities altogether by claiming your dues now, which I am in no position to pay. It's entirely your decision. Please decide wisely,"' recalls Suresh reliving those classic moments from many decades ago.

The creditors started holding animated discussions among themselves as JT patiently waited for their verdict, seemingly not bothered about the outcome. However, he knew with the instinct of a gambler playing for high stakes what the verdict would be. He just smiled when they said they would give him time and signalled for the party to begin. That was by no means the end of the story.

After the party, they were asked to come to Choice House the following day for settlement of dues. As they started trooping in to meet the boss, one at a time, they did not quite know what was in store.

He asked each creditor to meet him personally, gave them cheques for the respective amounts owed, against the promise that they would not cash those cheques. Instead, they would be paid their dues in instalments over the coming months and they were to return the cheques on completion of the payment. However, as far as the company's official balance sheet was concerned, all sundry debts stood cleared.

JT was thus able to tackle bigger issues on hand—there were larger debts to be settled with a few banks. He also had an export order on hand for ₹100 million which was the amount he had managed to get as advance from the Adani Group.

The only way out was to settle the bank dues, make sure his company was not declared a defaulter and line up suppliers for goods worth ₹100 million by getting them to offer him a credit line. Some would call it financial jugglery while others would settle for the term debt restructuring.

Arvin, too, remembers with amazement the days when about fifty vendors would turn up each day seeking payment but only two would be paid, while the rest would be sent back with the hope that it could be their turn next. Those days the often-heard refrain from JT was 'If I had the funds and could pay all my vendors, I wouldn't need managers. I need them to manage the shortage of funds.'

The total outstanding amount of ₹160 million to sundry creditors, which had rendered Choice Trading a negative net worth company, was whittled down to less than ₹90 million, one-tenth of the debt on account of Choice Air.

By August 1995, the company balance sheet reflected a positive position vis-à-vis its net worth. When we closed the financial year on 30 September, Choice Trading was no longer a case fit for the Board of Industrial and Financial Reconstruction, created under the Sick Industrial Companies Act, 1985, to bail out or even wind up sick companies. It was a remarkable escape, one that could safely be described as one where JT escaped financial ruin by the skin of his teeth.

The pain of Choice Air crash left tremors that easily lasted about three years. For the Choice management, this period offered something no B-School could ever teach: crisis management when faced with severe liquidity crunch. JT could be said to have found his own way to manoeuvre payment schedules while keeping his core business verticals ticking.

It was, in a sense, debt restructuring done in a very creative manner. Some would call it a fluke. Others would see a touch of genius in the way it was put together.

20

LIKE A PHOENIX

IF THE DEBT PORTFOLIO OF CHOICE TRADING HAD SCALED ₹900 million, an amount that was in those days considered to be extremely high, perhaps in today's value terms guided by inflation, could be the equivalent of well over half a billion rupees! And if the intangibles are taken into account, JT feels it was more in the vicinity of ₹2.5 billion.

Hence, one could not really blame the local community, including a few of his friends, for writing the epitaph of JT as an entrepreneur. If there was a betting culture prevailing in Kochi those days and the punters were taking bets on JT pulling through this crisis, the odds stacked against JT would indeed have been very high.

As weeks turned into months and months into years, there seemed to be no end in sight for the troubles that beset the Choice Group following its airlines debacle. It was like the organization was battling the threat of multiple organ failure. The problems encompassed the company's financials, production efficiency, cash flows and payment schedules. The worry lines got deeper as much for the banks that had offered loans to Choice as they did for dozens of sundry creditors whose payments were overdue.

Adding to the woes from the vagaries of seafood exports, a negative outlook pervading the real estate market had affected Choice Construction projects. Apart from the steady business provided by the shipping division, Choice School, though a non-profit operation, was going great guns, bringing that desperately needed sense of calm to JT, a beacon of light in a tunnel of darkness.

By then, the shrimp supplies in Nellore had dried up following delay in payments. A palpable sense of inertia gripped the Choice factory floors, regular shifts got compromised. With the net productivity falling, the invariable outcome was negative cash flow. In other words, with the supply–production chain slipping into a negative cycle, the factory with fixed overhead costs began acting as a drain on the already depleted reserves.

'As I saw it, JT was financially exposed on multiple fronts. All his verticals were like babies and he was not willing to abandon even the frail ones, even if it meant abandoning the robust ones as he nurtured the ailing babies back to health. He would divert funds from any one of his successful ventures to the one that was in the doldrums. It was always about survival, not consolidation,' comments Arvin about JT's penchant to keep his feet in more than one boat.

So, if you were looking in from the outside, there was no consistency in the way he ran his businesses. As a result, Choice Group was destined to undergo a snail-paced growth. It became a matter of survival for JT. Yet, he fought ferociously to keep his empire afloat, all the while exhorting his senior staff to make that extra push and turn things around. Despite the negative buzz, most customers were ready to cooperate; some suppliers expressed their readiness to sign up for deferred payment terms.

It was perhaps the confidence shown by these suppliers that kept the team alive. Two of the top customers from the US chipped in, agreeing to advance funds. The top management started slogging, many staying put in office up to eighteen hours a day!

Realizing only too well the serious financial condition of his company, JT decided to fix things that had imperilled the company. Loose ends started being tightened. The yield of shrimp after cooking and cooling that should have been 95 per cent had fallen to 85 per cent during JT's period of infatuation with the airlines project.

That alone was bleeding the company by a staggering $10,000 per consignment to the US. Reversing this operational deficiency was the first step. Soon, the cash flow improved and the suppliers started getting prompt repayments. The customers and suppliers, along with the main creditor, State Bank of India, joined the rebuilding process.

Sundaram Finance's Suresh vividly recalls the 1996–97 period when he was tasked by his managing director in Chennai with keeping a close watch over the Choice Group to recover their debt. 'Our exposure to Choice was only about ₹20 million. There were other creditors like the State Bank of India, Industrial Development Bank of India and Apple Finance. The lead creditor was exposed to the tune of ₹650 million, where the group's equity was pledged against the debt. I used to track the financial transactions of Choice as my cousin Usha was the company secretary there,' he says.

Those were the days when shipping used to be hugely profitable, earning up to 40 per cent returns but all those earnings were going into servicing the massive debt created by Choice Air. JT was saddled with the unenviable task of balancing the persistent pressure from all his creditors on the one hand and diverting available funds as working capital to keep his businesses alive. This was necessitated by the ninety-day fund flow cycle that was the norm in the seafood industry, though JT was in no position to withstand such a three-month cycle. It was pretty much a Catch-22 situation.

He met the financial institution heads one after the other, persuading them to choose an extension of payment time. He argued his case that opting for legal proceedings would be only self-defeating. With this masterstroke, JT proved two things. That he was a maverick at wriggling out of tight corners and a genius at making funds stretch.

The Choice Group, like many medium-sized enterprises, used to face regular cash flow problems. The group's liquidity rarely seemed sufficient to service old loans and debts as funds had to be utilized for ongoing operations. The group had the luxury of tapping resources in one area to offset negative cash flow in another.

While there were many like Arvin who even today feel JT did himself no favour by getting involved in multiple verticals, Suresh reiterates that there was always a flip side to this argument, 'I am convinced Choice School provided him much comfort as it began accepting more students and with it, interest-free deposits which would remain with him for a long period, till the students graduated Class 12.' Here, Suresh was delving into the mechanics of cash flow adjustments that he felt may have bailed out JT many a time.

The subtext to this story began playing out in 1997 when the world braced for the Asian Currency Crisis which played havoc with the Indian economy. The rupee lost its value against the US dollar and almost touched fifty. All Asian currencies had lost value then. During the crisis, India was encouraging large groups to participate in increasing exports.

The momentum of the Indian economic liberalization that began in the early 1990s was perhaps benchmarked best by a series of decisions by the Ministry of Commerce and Industry. To be more specific, these measures were envisioned by the mandarins at the directorate general of foreign trade in the H-wing of Udyog Bhavan in New Delhi.

If exports soon began setting the tone of a country whose commercial activities were weighed down by imports, the logistics was provided, initially by a clutch of Export Processing Zones, which were bolstered by the dozens of Special Economic Zones that soon began mushrooming across the length and breadth of the country. Lending strength to this forward thrust in the realm of exports were the export houses.

But the real traction came in the form of Trading Houses and Star Trading Houses, the latter getting further defined as Super Star Trading Houses. Naturally each category came with a clutch of incentives. To be deemed an Export House, the minimum shipment or FOB had to be ₹220 million, that of Trading House ₹1,120 million, Star Trading House ₹5,600 million and Super Star Trading House ₹11,680 million. It did not take long for nearly 80 per cent of all exports from India to be handled by these trading houses. Many such trading houses would issue subcontracts to shipping agents to achieve their target, Choice was one such beneficiary.

On completing the export obligation, funds began flowing. It was owing to the initiation of a new policy in banks, introduced by the Reserve Bank, for a one-time settlement.

After disposing of non-performing assets, the Choice Group still held a reserve position of a few million.

Between the 30 per cent write-off and transfer of reserve funds to service debt, the banks led by SBI were ready to do business with Choice again. Thus, by 2000, only four years after being hit by the Choice Air debacle, the company's debt burden had got whittled down phenomenally, from ₹900 million to ₹400 million.

Yet, ill fortune continued to plague Choice. The currency crisis worsened and India was concerned about the depreciating value of the Indian rupee against the US dollar which would adversely affect the imports, especially that of crude oil. The Reserve Bank of India supported the depreciating rupee by pressuring exporters to repatriate funds at a faster pace.

Till then, it was acceptable that exporters could give credit to importers for up to 180 days and hence the Choice Group used to ship goods to its subsidiary in the US, availing the 180-day window. A policy U-turn by the Reserve Bank of India, shrinking the credit period to only 90 days and imposing a 17 per cent penalty for default of the new rule, was an unkind cut for most exporters. Once again, Choice was at the receiving end, being forced to pay ₹60 million as penalty.

For JT, who had invested blood, sweat and tears to bring his company out of a potential debt trap, this was a severe blow. It looked as if the light that he saw at the end of the tunnel was once again being replaced by darkness.

When all seemed lost, he decided to go for a top-down restructuring of the Choice Group. But that could not be done unless he decided to take on one man, whose company was benefiting big time in the US, even while JT was bearing the financial brunt to keep his export commitments from the Nellore factory alive—John Z. Blazevich and Contessa.

The agreement Choice signed with Contessa had many layers to it. The American company was to be responsible for a total buyback from the Choice Nellore plant. But that came with a few riders. Blazevich's company would advance almost 80 per cent of the container cost. But that was only a notional payment as it would then start deducting many variables from the amount.

This would include interest or capital servicing cost, opportunity costs that would factor in the day of the product landing in the US and reduce a certain percentage for each day's delay. Eventually, the book profits that came solely from black tiger shrimp exports would evaporate for Choice. Instead, it would fetch Contessa huge margins once the consignment landed in the US. The deal was loaded heavily in favour of Contessa.

'It was not easy for me. But I decided to part ways with John as I realized I was not treated fairly. Here I was, providing him with the raw material for his Contessa brand of goods. He turned on his marketing skills to sell my product under his brand name. His cash register was ringing non-stop, whereas I was struggling to make ends meet. Our deal was heavily loaded in his favour; the decision on how much I would be paid for my shrimp consignments from Nellore was solely his,' says JT.

It was a tough call to make but JT decided it was critical for his survival to somehow wriggle out of this arrangement and try to start his own brand in the US. This time, he promised himself there would be no wild goose chases. It was his resolve to rein himself in while spotting opportunities to make a few dollars more. There was no way he was going to go berserk as he would have in the past.

It was almost as if JT was growing into the shoes of his one-time mentor, John Z. Blazevich. The maverick Jose was nowhere in sight, as JT started shaping himself into another Blazevich, minus the evident fault lines that brought his once-upon-a-time mentor to his knees.

21

THE BLAZEVICH PUZZLE

PERHAPS NO OTHER PERSON HAS INFLUENCED JT AS MUCH as the flamboyant Czech immigrant turned American tycoon John Z. Blazevich, in more ways than one. The first and lasting impact on JT's mind was the influence of his father whose thinking subtly impacted his thought process.

Other than that, two others played their roles in shaping his aspiration, though only in a limited sense—first Dhurvendra Prakash Goel or DP who opened his eyes to what all he could achieve in the material world and then Douglas Tilden of US Lines who introduced him to the art of grooming himself as a man of the world—how to present himself, communicate effectively and entertain naturally.

However, it was Blazevich who became the yardstick with which JT measured success. Even to this day, a few tell-tale signs of this adulation have left an indelible mark on his personality, completely altering his lifestyle forever. The power that this naturalized American held over JT was so strong that his one goal was to become another Blazevich. This enchantment with JZB lasted for almost two decades.

'Yes, John was my role model. He lived in Hollywood, led a dream life rubbing shoulders with elegant people, owned private jets, and was making tonnes of money. So, there I was, looking up to him, revelling in the role as his main supplier from India, but losing money all the time. I was getting sucked into his world, travelling in a private jet to London, getting to see an opulent lifestyle that I could not afford. He knew it,' JT recollects his early days in the US and how he was hugely influenced by Blazevich.

It took JT a while to pull himself out of the quicksand that was the JZB charm. But soon, he went on to turn the tables on his mentor. By then, it was too late for Blazevich.

Says JT, 'Those were the days that I convinced myself, there was nothing sinful in buying $1,000 shirts, trousers, $2,000 shoes and $10,000 watches. To put things in perspective, I debate with myself many times before splurging $500 on a set of drums that I like, given my passion for drumming. But those days, it was all about reinventing myself as the Indian version of JZB.'

When he decided to launch branded shrimp in the US with the label Tastee Choice, there was much scepticism all round. Soon, JT was breaking his head, trying to get some space on the US supermarket shelves. Blazevich kept blocking him all the way. Having learnt all about the niceties of marketing from the man who owned the mighty Contessa brand, he decided to try his hand at going retail with Shop Rite, the largest supermarket chain in New Jersey.

'My first meeting with Shop Rite's director Robert Cerullo was a disaster. Yet, I kept going back to Cerullo, reiterating all the reasons why he should give me shelf space, but to no avail. There were occasions when I would get reduced to tears after hearing his standard response: meet me after six months. My frustration grew and doubts began creeping in if I was not too hasty in dumping Contessa, which at least gave me assured sales,' he adds.

JT's persistence eventually wore down Cerullo who allowed him to meet his senior management and tell his associate, 'Gary, give him a shot, let's see what he does.' By the end of the year, Tastee Choice had found space on the shelves of Shop Rite. There were days when JT would take his entire family to some of the Shop Rite outlets and distribute the Tastee Choice shrimp to US customers. He still had a long way to go but the battle for the shelf had begun.

At that point of time, in early 2002, no one would have backed Tastee Choice which was pitted against the then market leader Contessa, and that too in the latter's home turf. It was the typical David slaying Goliath story. It took JT some time to digest, let alone savour the monumental feat he had pulled off. It was one of those rare victories of the underdog.

'I had actually done it! The impact of getting Tastee Choice on the US supermarket shelf had to be seen to be believed. Tastee Choice and Contessa were sitting side by side. I felt I had achieved the impossible. Honestly, I had always wanted to be like Blazevich, flamboyant, classy, rich. Sure, I could not be tall like him, he was 6 feet 2 inches while I was all of 5 feet 7 inches. I never could own a $50 million mansion in Beverly Hills, could not even dream of a private jet, nor being chauffeured around in stretch limousines,' JT walks down the memory lane.

By late 2003, he had begun toying with the plan to follow John and Contessa into the meal kit food segment. Many cautioned him about the pitfalls of stepping into the highest rung of the frozen food ladder. Among others, he also spoke to Orlando Pipolo, who was the production head at Contessa, before it went bust.

'I still remember his response: "Amigo, forget it. This is a game for the big boys. You don't fit in." I am not entirely sure whether I took his mocking tone in the right spirit. I think it went some way to reinforce my decision to become a big boy. Soon, Orlando returned home, to Argentina and I came away to India, the plan temporarily on hold,' he recalls.

Less than a year passed. JT, who had become a jury member for a film festival, was watching an 8 a.m. screening in Kavitha Theatre in Kochi when he received a call from Argentina. It was from Orlando who wished to confirm whether JT was still serious about the plan to start making meal kits. That was sometime in late 2004 or early 2005.

Orlando came on board and they started a small assembling unit for meal kits in Kochi, with women manually packing the kits. The Americans did not take to food manufactured and packed in India. By 2006, it was time to wind up the project.

In 2008, Orlando came back to JT with the proposal that they start a meal kit manufacturing unit in the US. By 2010, we started off Tastee Choice, US, from a rented facility in Quaker Town, Pennsylvania, with Orlando heading the unit.

'John was furious and predicted it would shut down in a year. He sued Orlando, saying it was his recipe that was being used for my brand. That charge did not stick, though the judge reprimanded Orlando with a penalty. I had confirmation from people in the industry that he was neither imitating nor copying any of the products that were produced at Contessa while he was working there. And I made sure this was true,' says JT.

There was another significant development in 2010, one that rewrote the equation in the frozen food sector to some extent. John Blazevich was forced to file for bankruptcy, leading to an overall meltdown of his assets. His Beverly Hills villa was one of the many casualties as it was seized by a consortium of banks that had exposure in Blazevich's investments.

'Over the next few years, Tastee Choice began making serious noise in the meal kit circles, then dominated by Unilever and Nestlé. By 2015, our volumes and margins justified my decision to relocate to a much larger warehousing facility in Pittston, Pennsylvania. This was a city with some history of coal mining and a workforce comprising European immigrants. The real growth of Tastee Choice began in Pittston,' he adds.

Choice Canning, its exposure so far limited to shrimp, began considering a bigger platter. In the following years, it acquired a much more diversified portfolio by adding chicken, beef, lobster, crab and a few other items to its menu. It had been some journey since 1999 when Choice decided to part ways with Contessa, the company that offered them the buy-back arrangement from Nellore.

'There is no denying the crucial role played by John in transforming the frozen food industry by giving it a glamorous direction. He redefined a pretty dull business with dedicated marketing and branding to take the product to the customer. Coincidentally, Tastee Choice touched $40 million in 2021, which is approximately what Contessa had done in 2008,' explains JT, about one of the rare cases of an Indian company entering the highly competitive food business.

That is, however, only less than half the story as Tastee Choice accounts for only 40 per cent of the ready-to-eat meal kits rolled out from Choice Canning's Pittston plant. The lion's share, up to 60 per cent of the plant's production, is consumed by the American public under a slew of private brands, most of them popular in certain geographical spaces. They have no reason to know it is an Indian company that manufactures their favourite meal kits.

With several neighbourhood stores, including Shop Rite, the store in New Jersey and Stop & Shop stacking up labels like Wholesome Pantry, Gold Star, Nature's Promise, Bowl & Basket, which roll out from Pittston, it has been advantage Choice, all the way.

In other words, Tastee Choice is only one product that gets rolled out of the company's frozen food factory that employs over 100 people from the US labour force. The 50,000 square feet facility that includes a 35,000 square feet cold storage space, now caters to scores of American labels or brands.

Chances are high that when you buy a skillet meal off the shelves in any of the over 50,000 stores across the US, you could be eating a meal prepared at JT's Pittston factory of Choice Canning. It could be pasta with shrimp, chicken or beef, but he has reason to feel elated as his frozen food vertical is now rated among the top companies in the US in that segment.

JT always wanted to get into the finer aspects of sales, marketing and branding, which was clearly where the products gained maximum value-addition. That may be why he decided to create a brand that was his own, as he could not stand by and watch Contessa calling all the shots.

His decision to get into niche areas was beginning to pay off. According to Suresh, who still tracks major seafood manufacturers in and around Kochi, it was probably JT's preoccupation with getting into niche segments that dented the company's fortunes initially, before he could turn things around.

'It was this mindset that got him to concentrate on high-end housing at a later stage. He wooed affluent parents to his school with world-class infrastructure including air-conditioned classrooms and buses. It was no different from setting up the first five-star office in the city, complete with a cafeteria that was not inferior to any big hotel, with a pool table and a roof-top bar,' says Suresh, once again sketching a thumbnail of the man who had by then pulled Choice out of fiscal trouble.

Mohan Varma is in no doubt that JT was hugely influenced by Blazevich. At the same time, he always tried to get as much talent as he could manage into his corner.

'It would not have surprised me if JT had considered asking Blazevich to partner with Tastee Choice at a later stage in life. Because that is precisely what he did with the Randazzo brothers of Brilliant Seafood, once our major client in Boston. If at all he did that, it would be a sincere offer and not an insult as it may appear to an outsider,' says Varma with a bemused look.

Having taken on the Blazevich challenge and come out on top, JT knew that while he still cherished what he learnt from the consummate salesman, it would be prudent to keep him in his past. Once the financial controller of Choice, Varma shares an interesting insight into why JT in all probability maintained his distance from the Group's primary undertaking, seafood and allied activities, except during the kaara chemmeen harvest season.

'JT once confided in me that there was no glamour in the seafood sector as it was nothing but a commodity trade.

Probably taking a leaf out of Blazevich's book, he pulled all stops to bring glamour into whatever he did. Thus came about his engagement with shipping and the highs of the US Lines. Choice Air, if it had happened, would have taken his graph through the stratosphere, way bigger than what many of his contemporaries thought,' says Varma.

Sure, the graduation of Chemmeen Jose from the Madras days to Shrimp King has been complete. A crucial phase in this makeover exercise was his decision to consciously step into the shoes of the one man he once worshipped—John Z. Blazevich. Still the reality remained that his yearning to be known by virtue of a brand had only become a partial reality. Tastee Choice, at best, would account for only a fraction of his seafood trade.

The image of JT as an international citizen, the jet-setter with friends in high places could find one venue for mass propagation—Choice School. Apart from his time spent at the school, he continued to live like a recluse while visiting his home town.

22

MOZAMBIQUE MOZART

IF THERE IS ONE THING JT HAS PROVED TIME AND AGAIN IT is that he is a long-haul player, forever willing to wear out his competitors. At the same time, he has always been susceptible to the occasional adventure, underlined by his propensity to take risks.

It was in the early 1980s that young Jose Thomas, then in his mid-twenties, salvaged the cargo of a ship abandoned by its owners off the Indian coast all the way to Khartoum, fetching him a windfall gain of $800,000 from the Sudan government.

It took over a quarter century for him to consider Africa as a place where he could seek his fortunes, yet again. In 2008, he sought to an encore, this time landing in Mozambique's port town of Cabo Delgado province. Unlike salvaging a cargo, it was real hard work this time as he began seeking his pot of gold in black tiger shrimps from the African coastal villages.

Curiously, this was also the period when the US economy had entered a particularly dark phase. It began in 2007, peaked in 2008 and its repercussions consumed a good part of the global economy till 2010. The ripple effect, triggered by the collapse of Lehman Brothers, led to collateral damage that went way beyond real estate mortgages. Seafood proved to be no exception.

Amidst all this, consumption of shrimp was booming in the US and it was but natural that importers would look at fresh origins to source the raw material. Therefore, when a new buzz, cultivating black tiger shrimp in Africa, began doing the rounds, he simply couldn't resist the urge to go out and explore the possibilities.

For JT, who was clued into the ramifications of the ongoing economic meltdown, perhaps a degree more than many others, the possibility of any positive intervention to rejuvenate the market was like a bugle call. Soon, he was in talks with a big investor from South Africa who was willing to invest up to $50 million for shrimp processing and exporting factory in Mozambique, provided JT was willing to run it.

'I had this conversation with Willy Pabst, an industrialist with multiple ventures in Zimbabwe and South Africa, who wanted to partner with me for a black tiger shrimp processing plant in a place called Pemba, near Mozambique. All he wanted was for me to take charge of the processing and also buy the final product for the US market. He would make the majority investment, my exposure would be minimal. That was the deal,' he recalls the beginning of what he thought would be a life-changing venture.

'I was naturally tempted as the market for shrimp was expanding in the US. I began considering the possibilities, mentally counting the profits of entering a virgin territory. I did not discuss it with anyone, but decided to go for it after consulting my lawyer. Soon, I was in Johannesburg and the project was on,' adds JT of a venture that he expected would take him to a continent where he made his first fortune.

Pemba, world renowned for its virgin beaches, coral reefs as also the pristine waters that played home to whales and dolphins, became a potential raw material source for JT's aspirations. During the next couple of years, he did not see anything in and around Pemba that excited the tourists, including many planning their honeymoon getaways.

His focus was only on those who could be picked to work in the factory, right from peeling to cooking and processing the region's bounty—the black tiger shrimp. It helped that there was a flight to Pemba from Dar es Salaam twice a week. JT soon became so friendly with the captain that he would often share the cockpit space during these long flights.

He also would stay at a beach hotel in Pemba. There ended the fun part as he began yet another adventure. This time round, it was in a corner of the world where AIDS was almost as rampant as the common cold.

'I would continue to visit this province in Mozambique for the next three years. It became a part of my routine, spending up to a fortnight every thirty to forty days. Portuguese was the spoken language, the villagers were living in abject poverty, in mud-built cottages, there were many who were suffering from AIDS. However, my task was clear—Pemba was to pave the way for my secure future in the US,' recalls JT.

To lend perspective, his youngest son, Jacob, who was a toddler then, would tell his mother that she should forget about shopping from budget-friendly stores as his father was super rich with his new factory in Mozambique. To some extent, JT too believed he was set to repeat history, by hitting the jackpot a second time in Africa.

He could not be faulted for thinking along those lines as Pabst began pouring in the funds. Soon rolled in the machinery, everything imported into a region not known for industrial growth. JT had managed to recruit about 200 workers; no small feat as identifying healthy workers in a region known for its HIV positive population was extremely difficult.

He began overseeing their training, getting them on the same page about hygiene, which was a major challenge. The factory production started in just over a year. Container-loads of processed shrimp began getting exported to the US, the returns began flowing in, and things were going as per plan. JT even posted a couple of senior managers from his Kochi plant in Pemba in anticipation of a ramp-up in production.

'We were blindsided by an unforeseen political upheaval. There was a military coup in Mozambique and the military general in Cabo Delgado under whose protection Pabst and I got the factory running, was executed. A new militia took over. We literally had to run for our lives, abandoning our costly machinery and all our investment,' remembers JT with a shudder.

For Pabst and JT, the worst case scenario came true when the socio-economic situation in Mozambique began to spiral out of control in 2010. By September, unchecked inflation led to an unprecedented situation where thousands of local people started what later came to be known as food riots. Investors began abandoning the region as genuine fear for their lives trumped worries over material losses. To make matters worse, talks of an imminent military coup were in the air. Faced with a total breakdown of normalcy, Pabst and JT had no option but to abandon their thirty months worth of hard work and significant investment in favour of the lives of their staff. Later, it was heard that the local people ransacked the factory, with the costly machinery arguably getting sold as scrap.*

Pabst lost close to $50 million, of which $26 million was his personal investment while over $20 million was raised from some of his associates. There were quite a few professionals involved in the Pemba shrimp farming project like Patrick Wood and Marcus Moya, apart from a bunch of senior managers from Choice, India.

Catching up with Pabst in Cape Town took a while. Willy, as he prefers to be addressed, had one thing to say. That he would not like to be made to relive the only venture in his life that ended up as a failure. The onus of the failure falls on the corrupt government machinery that kept contaminating the shrimp farm and steadily stealing from the harvest, before the military coup finally oversaw the last rites of what was already a dying project. But he does not wish to go on record, pinning the blame on any one for the Pemba project going kaput.

Pabst, a European settler in Zimbabwe, who has in the past donned the hat of a gold miner in South Africa, refers to the Mozambique venture as a nightmare he wishes to forget. According to him the local officials kept themselves mired in the ashes of corruption. Willy Pabst is presently the owner of the world's largest privately owned game reserve, the 60,000 hectare Sango Wildlife Conservancy in Zimbabwe.

Busy running the most exotic wildlife parks and safari destinations complete with a lodge in the entire African continent, which by extension means the world, Willy, who is perhaps the largest land owner in Zimbabwe, reiterates

* 'Police say arrest 148 in Mozambique after food riots', Reuters,6 September 2010, https://www.reuters.com/article/ozatp-mozambique-protest-20100906-idAFJOE6850AM20100906>

his recollection of what was a horror show in Mozambique, which gave him sleepless nights for months together.

For a tycoon who has seen billions coming his way as he is into disinvesting from a bulk of his African projects, it is more than just about the loss of his personal funds in excess of $26 million. What still remains a thorn in his flesh is the way the Pemba shrimp farm was systematically run to ground over a thirty-month period, from 2008 to 2010.

What rankles most is he could see it happening but could do very little to help. Harvest after harvest comprising tonnes of shrimp got contaminated as those in power got into openly stealing from the produce. Though Willy was able to withstand the onslaught of corruption in all his other projects, the Mozambique project was an exception.

For Willy, this is a chapter he would prefer to forget as many of his employees lost their jobs, many lives were destroyed—the only failure in his long career as an entrepreneur.

Sure, by comparison JT got off cheap, having lost only $1 million but that was $1 million more than he could afford to lose. For someone, who was prepared to enrol local residents living under the threat of AIDS for a project that did not do as well as he anticipated, JT certainly had not bargained for a military coup!

In retrospect, one could always point out that JT did not factor in the tell-tale signs of insurgency and the presence of Boko Haram in Mozambique but then that is the case in many other African nations. The Pemba project clearly did not fully gauge the scope of corruption that was rampant in Mozambique as it was in many African nations.

Apart from the military coup annihilating the Pemba project and the corrupt local officials eroding the profitability of the facility, there was a third reality. Like many major projects, the Mozambique shrimp plant had an inherent flaw, which unfortunately for the principals was allowed to grow unchecked till it became a cancer that consumed its very foundation.

In the initial days, the hatchery was handled by a company run by Filipinos who also had a say in the way the shrimp farm was cultivated. After a few months, they began to take a side seat as the investors brought in their respective teams.

Pabst, a German national settled in Zimbabwe, brought in a bunch of Europeans with Latin American roots at the technical and operation level. JT brought in hand-picked men from his Indian factories. The workers were mostly uneducated women from Pemba who had precious little exposure to the concept of hygiene. Then there were the Mozambique government officials.

As the comfort level of the Filipinos started going out of the window, the hatchery-to-farm line started witnessing disruptions. Simply put, there were too many players in what soon became a boiling cauldron of ideas, technological inputs, supervisory guidelines and bureaucratic control. It was a disaster waiting to happen. The operating margins had started reflecting these disruptions months before the military coup blew the lid on the project.

Yes, investments still take place in countries that are not famous for their political stability. Counter-balancing the risk are prospects of high returns with lower capital outlays on account of cheap land and labour always proving to be a lure. Had he pulled it off, JT and Pabst would have been celebrated by the entire seafood industry as visionaries. But that was not to be.

In retrospect, was the Mozambique project in sync with carefully nurtured personality of JT? Not really. A good fourteen years had passed since the irrepressible Jose went for broke, bidding for a spot in the Indian skies, almost bringing down the Choice Group of companies.

By 2008, his quest for the fabled pot of gold had turned more cautious. This he did by finding a partner in Willy Pabst to bear the brunt of the damage when things went south in Mozambique.

Evidently, the reappearance of the irrepressible Jose resulted only in collateral damage to the Choice Group unlike in the past when the entire losses would be borne by the Choice Group's balance sheet one way or the other. That is because the mature persona of JT was in reasonable control of the proceedings, by roping in a partner to bear the bulk of the damages.

At the end of the day, it was a symphony comprising many nationals that ended up striking a note of discord. By then, JT had sharpened his risk mitigation skills, minimizing his monetary exposure while undertaking the high-risk Mozambique project. It was another matter altogether that the outcome was quite different for the hapless Pabst.

23

LAL–JOSE CAPERS

IN 2008, JUST AS JT'S FRENETIC PURSUANCE OF THE AMBITIOUS Mozambique project was getting played out along the African coast, his trips to his hometown began turning quite interesting. That was when acclaimed Malayalam film actor Mohanlal—celebrated across India for his effortless portrayal of hundreds of characters on the silver screen—entered his life in an emphatic manner.

With over 350 films in Indian cinema and a clutch of national and state awards under his belt, Mohanlal is one of the most popular faces in south India. Having straddled the southern film world like a colossus for the past four decades, Mohanlal had become a household name by the turn of the century. JT was no exception to the multitude of Keralites who wished to get up close and personal with Mohanlal. Unlike most others, a chance to do so fell into his lap some time in 2008.

It was actually another actor, Dileep, who made it all happen. The shooting of what was to become a runaway box-office hit, *Twenty 20,* had just begun. It was a rare film where Dileep, also the producer, persuaded the entire array of south Indian film stars—Mammootty, Mohanlal, Suresh Gopy, Jayaram—to become part of a rare multi-starrer.

While scouting for an ideal location for a crucial outdoor scene, Dileep's producer, Poduval, approached a manager at Choice House, the waterfront property that doubles as JT's office-cum-residence during the days when he was visiting India.

'I was not keen to let a film shoot happen in the artistically landscaped property that housed heritage structures. Yet, when I heard Poduval was waiting to meet me with a personal request from Dileep, I decided to hear him out,' reminisces JT.

Actually, there was another reason. JT had heard there was a very good chance that Mohanlal would be among the actors shooting on his property. JT asked Dileep's manager whether he could have some private time with Lal if the permission to shoot the film on his property was given. The answer was in the affirmative!

Soon, the shooting schedule of *Twenty 20* commenced in Choice House. The property owner kept his eyes peeled for the star to give him the promised private audience. JT eagerly waited for an opportune time, while Lal probably thought he had to keep the house owner satisfied so that the shoot would not be adversely affected. Little did either of them know then that this would be the beginning of a real friendship, its bonds strengthening with the passage of time.

They hit if off famously from day one. This paved the foundation for an unparalleled friendship that would last the test of time and geographical divide. One meeting between the super star and the maverick industrialist got the chemistry going. One must remember that while Mohanlal made friends quite easily, it was not the same for JT, who was known for shying away from society.

He recalls with genuine warmth how Lal, who when first introduced to his wife and children, got enthusiastically involved in trying to find the right match for JT's eldest daughter, who had just turned twenty.

'Lal effortlessly eased into the character of the matchmaker and suggested we should go for an alliance with the Baby Marine Ventures with whom he had close ties. He was quite emphatic while suggesting we should push for a marriage between my daughter and one of the boys from the Baby Marine family. That did not go to the next stage as the boy was already engaged, but Lal and I became thick friends, and our families also became very close. And these ties have only emerged stronger as we are close to celebrating fourteen years of our friendship,' says JT.

There were two tangible takeaways from the Lal–Jose friendship. The first one, JT PAC or the Jose Thomas Performing Arts Centre, came up within a year, in 2009. A permanent auditorium was offered by JT as Kochi's nearest possible answer to the question posed by the nearly four-and-a-half-decades-old Soorya Dance & Music Festival in the state capital.

JT PAC was founded on 26 February 2009, with Mohanlal as its chairman and JT as president. The performing arts centre boasted of world-class acoustics inside the Choice School complex with a seating capacity of 700. The building of Brand JT and by extension, the advancement of the Choice Group of companies, had to be structured somewhat indirectly. Because shrimp processing and export which was core activity did not offer much scope for image building at that point of time.

The Rhyme by Soorya Krishnamoorthy was the first show performed at the theatre. Later that year, Mohanlal played Prospero in a Malayalam version of *The Tempest*, and Bhima in a play titled *Chayamukhi*. Since then, JT PAC has hosted about 500 shows with renowned artists like Pankaj Udhas, Udit Narayan, Shankar Mahadevan, Pandit Hari Prasad Chaurasia, Ustad Amjad Ali Khan and Naseeruddin Shah performing there.

In 2012, the arts centre organized a four-day dance festival titled 'Parampara' in which Padma Shri recipient Madhavi Mudgal, Bharati Shivaji, Saswati Sen and Rama Vaidyanathan were among those who performed at the centre.

As the pandemic period snuffed out all cultural activities in most parts of the country, JT PAC too has ground to a halt. Now, JT feels it has more chance of survival in the US, among the Indian settlers starved of a permanent venue to host renowned artistes from India. It also holds a mirror to his mind that is now inclined to spend more time in the US than in India.

JT does not have even an iota of doubt whether Lal would become a patron of the US version of JT PAC, should such a venture come up. 'If I decide to start a new innings for JT PAC in the US, I am sure Lal would be as excited as I. We are soul mates, having been through thick and thin. Why, once we even encountered death together,' JT says with a wide grin.

JT goes on to share the broad contours of a bizarre incident from 2017, when they were together in Japan on what he describes as a bonding holiday to South-east Asia:

'We were received at the Narita International Airport by Nakagawa San who was the head of Choice, Tokyo. We had flown in from Singapore and soon made our way to Kyoto.

We looked forward to an enjoyable stay there before proceeding to Osaka, and then flying out to Seoul,' recalls JT.

They rounded off their day in Kyoto with a geisha dinner at the hotel near the railway station. The dinner went fine, neither of them had much to drink, probably as they were exhausted after a busy day. They proceeded to their rooms for an early night as the train next morning was at 6.30 a.m.

'I went down to the lobby at 5.55 a.m., surprised to find Lal was not waiting for me, as is his nature. By 6.15 a.m., after many furtive glances at the lift which failed to bring Lal, I knew we would miss our train. I was getting restless and after fifteen minutes I started calling Lal on his phone but there was no answer,' remembers JT about an incident that he has rarely mentioned to anyone back home.

Though it was cold outside, by then JT was sweating profusely, as his imagination started running wild, some of the worst-case scenarios flashing in his mind.

'That was one time when I was gripped by stress and outright fear so early in the day. I just could not get rid of this feeling that he was lying unconscious on the ground, may be after a heart attack. And it had happened during my watch, I was somehow responsible. How could I explain this to anyone, let alone his family? My body was paralysed, my mind not unlike a runaway train when there was no response from Lal to my banging on his door, shouting out his name,' JT recalls that one hour many years ago in Japan with a mixture of dread and amusement.

Soon he convinced the front desk manager to break open the door as it was locked from inside and their pass key would not work. As he did not have the courage to accompany them into the room, JT went back to the lobby.

'Imagine my relief when the hotel staff returned a few minutes later and said Lal was fast asleep, oblivious to all the commotion he had caused,' says JT, struggling to put the anti-climax in words. 'As Lal came down in a hurry, the first thing I told him was that I would never travel with him again. Of course that was said in the heat of the moment. We have travelled together many times since then,' he adds.

Over the next four years, their friendship strengthened further as Lal often joined JT in his culinary adventures. While he has gone on to take certificate courses offered by famous chefs in Thai and Italian cuisine, Lal has remained a keen learner from his friend and often surprises his wife Suchitra by taking over the family kitchen on many occasions.

The past few years have seen his Club House, which also doubles up as a bar, recreation centre as well as a culinary hub, play host to his many experiments with Lal in the finer aspects of both oriental and continental cooking. Adding a splash of colour to such evenings, JT plays the drums in accompaniment even as one of the most popular actors in India belts out a few songs.

Sure, these get-togethers take place only a few times a year. However, JT's passion for entertaining guests means he has a steady flow of film actors, directors, playback singers, musicians, bureaucrats, politicians, leading surgeons and media friends attending his Kochi durbaar with fair regularity.

The leading name in the list would always be Mohanlal as he also finds time to join the famous Lal–Jose cooking sessions, both donning the chef caps. This would be followed by Lal getting into the groove, singing songs that not many would otherwise get to hear—popular tunes in Malayalam, Hindi and English. JT would be at the drums. The sessions would go on and on, late into the night.

Then there are evenings when the Club House turns into a melting pot of entrepreneurial concepts and practices. Youngsters would come up with project plans, with JT not playing the role of a mentor, but sometimes even turning into an angel investor and financing a few such start-ups.

Unknown to the outside world, the Choice House has been one of the most unconventional start-up hubs in Kerala, maybe India. It is anybody's call if JT would want to maintain this idyllic waterfront property spread over a few acres after his headquarters has shifted to Chennai. JT says he would try to reinvent his durbaar in New Jersey by converting what was originally a barn into a club house.

Yet, it will not be quite the same as the one he still has up and running in his hometown, the waterfront property, is a favoured destination for many across India. Each time JT chooses to spend a few weeks in India, the Choice House gets filled up fast. This is a ritual that is spread across a few weeks, till he returns to the US.

24

TAIL WINDS

14 SEPTEMBER 2020 WILL ALWAYS BE A RED-LETTER DAY FOR JT. That was the day he declared to the world that he was getting a move on, that he had arrived. It was as much a declaration of his joining the high table where only the well-heeled are allowed entry.

It was on that day he bought the 1890-built, 6,250 square feet Dutch mansion spread over an acre of prime property on Hillcrest Avenue, Summit, New Jersey. It was one of the best investments he has made at around $3 million as its value has shot up with the US real estate market going ballistic.

It has been quite a journey since moving into the small, rented apartment in Queens, New York, in the mid-1980s with his wife and two toddlers. Then came his first own house in Monroe, about an hour's drive from New York City, a house that he held on to till the middle of 2021. This was followed by his twenty-second floor waterfront apartment at 77, Hudson Street, Jersey. Thereafter, he went on to buy a villa in Westfield Town, only about 20 km from Manhattan.

Curiously, Hilcrest Avenue is the first property he has purchased in the name of his company, Choice Canning Company Inc., USA. The rest of his realty purchases, after his first rented apartment in Queens, New York, have all been in his name.

JT has moved through a few office spaces too. Perhaps the most famous one was 19, Rector Street Office, as it was situated quite close to the New York Stock Exchange and the Wall Street as also the World Trade Centre office. There was also the one in Edison located amid the Indian hub in New Jersey. But the place that has witnessed Choice fortunes really grow is the one at 15 Exchange Place in Jersey City overlooking Hudson river, right across Rockefeller Park, New York.

The luxury of his Exchange Place office and the laidback lifestyle of his Summit residence came after a few decades of real struggle to gain a foothold in the slippery slope that defines corporate America. Even his harshest critics now admit that JT has finally arrived in the US.

A bulk of that success has come recently, mostly as a direct offshoot of the pandemic-induced lifestyle changes. It made a major impact in the bottomline of Choice US as one of those changes was the average American's eating habits.

'It is not that nothing good happened in my life either personally or professionally in the past few years. Looking back, things were going well, barring the odd bumps but there was nothing remarkable taking place in my life. In a way, I am thankful for this phase of no disruptions. Sure, there have been no action-packed incidents that make good story material but my US investments grew the fastest during the pandemic years,' says JT with a shrug.

Alok Modani, financial controller of Choice Canning Inc, gives an insight into how the US story developed, 'The Choice US operations have been clocking a fast growth rate. From $27 million in 2009, the year I joined the company, to $200 million in just twelve years, the pace has been phenomenal. And from $200 million to $300 million, the trajectory will be much faster. What has worked in our favour is India has outstripped other countries as raw material sources for seafood including Indonesia, Vietnam and Thailand. For many years, 70 per cent of our raw material came from India and 30 per cent from the rest of the world. Right now, almost 100 per cent of our shrimp comes from India.'

Make no mistake, it is in the US that JT feels he is at home as a part of the segment he refers to as the 'White Collar Avenue'. All this, while he is gearing up to take his ready-to-eat-meal product line to some of the hitherto untested parts of Europe, like Italy and the UK.

'I feel we are finally to realize my dream of transforming Choice into a multi-billion dollar company, provided we are able to look at the inorganic growth route. That would also help Choice look beyond the US markets, expanding our market into Europe and even Asia. Thus, it is going to be a double-edged growth mantra—more products, bigger market. We have to scale up on both fronts,' says JT.

These are more than mere plans; they have reached project activation stage, with JT once again crisscrossing continents to make things happen at his pace. Sure, one of his sons may tag along but ultimately all decisions are his alone to make, there is not much delegation, it is a complete hands-on show by JT. That is a character trait that he finds difficult to alter.

Having been scalded a few times, JT does not wish to leave anything to chance, so he feels compelled to handhold Operation Choice Global as his own baby. He is fully convinced either Choice Trading India or Choice Canning US would be in a position to go public by the first half of 2026, but the expansion plans will not hold till then.

Even though JT was fully focused on the US market, at the bottom of his heart he always wanted to do business with Japan—one country whose work ethics he revered. He feels his mission is still incomplete unless he can build bridges with the hitherto elusive Japanese.

Thus, it was with a sense of great pride that he closed a significant business deal with the seafood division of Marubeni Corp, a very exciting project. It was a win–win for both.

'However, to my utter dismay, my Cochin team did not perform to the expectation of Marubeni and they decided to cancel the contract and proceed with someone else in India. The main reason cited was delay in delivery. The Japanese are firm on no compromise on commitment. Unfortunately, in India it is the other way round. My team, for whatever reason, did not ship the goods on schedule, and everything fell apart.'

JT simply could not believe that his long string of misfortunes with the Japanese had once again resulted in considerable loss of face for him. Consequently, he decided to atone for his mistake and try to beard the lion in its den.

So, in January 2020, he flew to Tokyo, checking in at Imperial Hotel as he had done many times in the past. Then started his long wait for the senior management team of Marubeni for the appointment at the mutually agreed upon time.

'To be frank, I went there to plead guilty with my Japanese friends because I had failed to deliver what I had promised. It was an act of atonement on my part as they had invested both time and money by sending their team for a reconnaissance trip when they were tasked with doing the due diligence of my India operations. I had made certain projections and my team could not deliver to the level I expected,' confides JT.

At the end of the day, it was his failure. The Marubeni team arrived two hours late for the meeting, which contradicted their insistence on punctuality. Then they refused to take JT out, which they had always done in the past.

'It was evidently a snub, driving home their displeasure. I was fully mindful that I deserved this treatment, their insult. It shook me up pretty hard but I did not yield by showing any anger. Instead, I decided that I would not give up on my dream,' adds JT, not bothering to hide his hurt.

Life is but a series of events strung together by the thread called fate. Tastee Choice became such a spectacular success that JT was approached by another multi-billion dollar Japanese food and beverages major, seeking an alliance.

'I got a mail from the New Jersey State Commerce Department saying they had been approached by a Japanese company, seeking information about Choice US and our meal-kit brand, Tastee Choice. I have to withhold the company's identity on account of the non-disclosure agreement we have signed as they go through the evaluation of our company. Now, this is poetic justice, the fact that a Japanese company has come wooing us. At this juncture, a stake sale or even the total hiving off of Tastee Choice does would not be a fiscally prudent move, so we are not selling. Yet, I now have a sense of how big we can make this brand,' he points out.

The Japanese food major has done JT a favour by systematically pouring over the books of accounts and the sales figures of Tastee Choice. Add to that the due diligence of its supply chain and production facilities in Pittston, Pennsylvania, by lawyers and bankers, and what JT has been given on a platter is a basic brand valuation of Tastee Choice at zero cost.

What this valuation process has provided JT with is considerable elbow room to engage with future buyers even as the volumes and the geographical reach of the brand keeps going up. JT knows he is sitting on millions of dollars from a fledgling venture he started in the face of severe opposition from top players like Blazevich.

'It is our call as to when we wish to leverage the volumes we have created, the shelf space we have taken up in stores across the US, some under our brand name but a lot more by supplying the product, complete with their brand name from our manufacturing base in Pittston, Pennsylvania. I am in no hurry to enter into any agreement or offload equity in a rush as the ball is in their court this time, unlike in the past when it was invariably I who was out courting possible suitors,' says JT.

Given Choice Canning's exposure in the ready-to-eat frozen food segment, there are many things it is capable of achieving in terms of last-mile connectivity. With India remaining the top shrimp producer in the world for the past three years, the group is also revamping its Indian operations on a major scale.

'The turnover from our existing branded food line is slated to touch $100 million by 2024. This figure would see a considerable spike once new products hit the shelves and our retail network expands. We are on course to achieve both. We are going ahead with the introduction of an entire range of breaded food products pretty soon. On the cards are an array of products like dumpling, ravioli, empanada and even samosa, with meat and seafood filling options,' reveals JT.

By his own admission, there are many industrialists from his home state who are wealthier than he is or ever could be. All his life has been a constant reminder of this reality and he has never been blind to it but it was always his claim that his life has been far more interesting and certainly more adventurous than theirs.

Therefore, after a long time in the wilderness, when JT is finally getting a chance to get a toehold in a category that is defined by wealth, it is hard to miss the gleam of satisfaction in his eyes. Particularly as his frozen food has been flying off the shelves in thousands of stores in the US. There is no second-guessing the fact that the Covid-19 pandemic gave a boost to his frozen food product line which has been a boon for families that want to step out less and can bank on frozen food to help them get through the difficult times.

JT sold his yacht with a plan to replace the 66-feet yacht with one in the 100-feet category. Having given up on his dream to own a shipping line or private airline company, JT may settle for his own chopper. It's not quite the same as owning a jet, but he has learnt to be more realistic and prudent.

'I now enjoy liquidity worth millions of dollars, something I never had the luxury of having ever before. This has allowed me a breather, getting me to consider building a theatre for performing arts in New Jersey, quite like the one in Kochi. I have played host for and entertained so many well-known personalities in India with whom I have wined, dined and sang. Maybe I will get to do that all over again in the US,' he says, raising his glass in a toast.

If and when the Tastee Choice deal does come through, JT will get to enjoy the kind of liquidity he has never enjoyed before. Strange as it may sound, he is unsure how happy he will be in that comfort zone. Just as he was not sure how complacent he would have got if the US Lines debacle had not happened, keeping him snug in a cocoon of security but with very few challenges in life.

However, welcoming a period of stability that only enhanced liquidity can bring, would be his wife and children. They would happily settle for JT going for a bigger yacht or even a private jet, as long as he keeps away from high-risk ventures. Surely, they can only hope as the very process of resolving the Jose–JT debate is replete with complexities where nothing can be taken for granted.

'The consolidation phase has been quite successful, now the time is ripe for expansion. Seafood export enjoys synergy with the meal kit segment, though it is but forward integration, providing a strong core for lateral growth. All my existing verticals are built around Choice US which is doing a quarter of a billion. We are very much on course to touch the billion-dollar mark in 2025–26,' says JT.

He is fully aware that there are many others of Indian origin who have achieved all that and more in a much shorter period of time. But then he has always been a votary of taking his time and space to reach his destination.

As he consciously wears the persona of a man at ease hobnobbing with his peers at the corporate high table, JT is getting quite comfortable with his image makeover. As a resident of Summit in New Jersey and employer of a few hundred US citizens, the youngster who gazed out at the Arabian Sea in his hometown, is satisfied. Yes, it has taken him a while to get to where he is now, but he has done it.

It is with some pride that JT reiterates he has never jumped lines to get where he is. However, when he says he never broke the law, never solicited, never did anything unethical, and still could build an organization which he is very proud of, there is a flip side to it.

By opting to ignore the business ecosystem in India that was built on the 'licence raj', his conscious decision to take the ethical route has cost him quite a lot. Otherwise, his company could have grown much faster, as he himself admits.

'I have no regrets. I am perfectly happy with what has been done by Choice, as a business entity, the right way,' he declares.

25

BACK TO THE FUTURE

THE PANDEMIC AND RESULTANT SOCIAL DISTANCING protocols had resulted in a huge surge in demand from the American families for ready-to-eat meal kits. One of the main beneficiaries has been Choice Canning, US. As this lifestyle seems set to last a couple of years more, a number of companies are keen to climb onto this bandwagon. That means Choice has no option but to get a move on. In a bid to remain ahead in this race, JT has trained his guns on two things—introducing new products to their menu and widening their reach into new markets.

Choice Canning, US, will now be spreading wings into Europe and also Asia. JT has also made clear he will henceforth concentrate only on new projects. The writing on the wall is fairly clear—the next three years could witness frenetic activity, which is coming after almost a decade-long period of consolidation. All that will require some fundamental changes in the way his Indian business is conducted.

'What is on my plate now is one big target, quite achievable, as we are already on course. By 2025–26, I aim to achieve two things. The first is to take Choice Trading operations in India public by going in for an IPO in 2025. I simply cannot rest till this goal is achieved,' confides JT, well aware he has delayed getting there by a few years.

The real challenge that faces JT is how the various verticals and multiple geographical locations can be dovetailed into an efficient, future-friendly matrix where the Next Gen is given a blueprint on how to take the Jose Thomas legacy forward. Or in other words, it is all about getting into the nuanced intricacies and complexities of freezing his succession plan.

Historically, JT has had two things working against his empire-building aspirations. On many occasions, when he thought things were going smooth, the support team would invariably let him down. He has been chary of admitting this to be his Group's faultline, often resulting in major setbacks to his extravagant plans to take the Choice Group into the big league.

Clearly, those engaged in the discussion of JT's retirement plans would be advised to put those on hold for another four years because there is no way he is going to entrust the most crucial part of his future plans to anyone, either within or outside his family.

It is not that he does not like to be prepared for the future and he is aware of the need for a good succession plan being put in place to take his hard-earned legacy forward. It is not unlike a well-rehearsed baton exchange, with perfect synchronization, so that the likelihood of any unforeseen hurdles gets minimized.

JT was never the one to actively consider retirement. Nothing could be further from his thoughts. Sure, he would like to visit Paris and see the Eiffel Tower. He certainly would not mind a visit to Rome, maybe a detour to the Vatican topped off with an audience with the Pope.

But one should also be prepared for JT trying to get his seafood product line endorsed by a famous French chef in Paris, with an exclusive supply contract with one of the better restaurant chains along the banks of River Seine. Nor if he tries to convince a cardinal or two that the one thing missing for the visitors to the Sistine Chapel and St Peter's Basilica is the genuine shrimp, all the way from India. Because, these are the kind of things he is capable of.

The semi-retirement plans his children had been planning for a while will now be put on hold. 'Not that I was ever a part to these plans,' confides JT, with a grin. 'What I see coming up for the Choice Group is a couple of years of international engagement, where a whole new range of food products will get into the food shelves of stores in many countries. We will be truthfully claiming the label of a multi-national company,' he adds.

JT, more than anyone else, would be the first to admit, that this is one race where he cannot afford to take any risks. His children are cautious, refusing to be drawn into openly discussing their father's retirement plans.

'The conversations at home are mostly about starting new ventures and how things are going to be in the days to come. He likes to be prepared for whatever the future holds and wishes us to be equally ready,' says his daughter Priya.

'We feel it is time all five of us started getting involved professionally as would the board of directors of any other company. It is not in any sense an attempt to get our dad to retire. We know he will never do that. Neither do we want him to,' adds his second daughter Divya.

'We want to groom ourselves as worthy of our dad's trust, given the passion and energy with which he has almost single-handedly nurtured multiple projects. Right now, it is all centred round one man—JT! We have to take it to the next level where the Group ventures run on their own momentum,' adds Elsa, the youngest daughter.

'I now shoulder most of the responsibilities to consolidate our India interests. My brother Jacob handles a bulk of the sales activities in the US. Now, we all feel it is time all of us got involved in the entire gamut of the company's activities,' asserts Thomas.

For a person whose forte has never been delegation of core functions, JT has found what he feels is a winning formula. While he has delegated some critical management functions like sales and project execution to his sons, key portfolios like finance and IT have been farmed out to professionals, of course, all under his watchful eye.

Jacob is quite like his father. Many go as far as to say that he is a maverick in the making. He heads the sales in New York, where he closes big contracts. In a sense, he is the powerhouse, setting the pace of the group's US business. JT sees in Jacob a glimpse of the go-getter he was in his younger days.

'But neither Jacob nor Thomas and most definitely not the girls, know what it is to have the very foundation of their business swept away from under their feet. Unless they live through such a crisis and survive, I cannot say for sure they are ready to do business without my help,' says JT.

That lesson may well be out of the curriculum, so to speak, since JT is sure he will never allow such a crisis to develop as long as he is at the helm.

Meanwhile, it was his long periods of absence from India during the pandemic that really forced the hand of JT into pushing his son, Thomas, into donning the role of India head. JT had decided that he was going to spend more time in the US apart from scoping out new ventures in Europe and Asia.

Thomas was suddenly required to do things which normally his father would have and has been thrust into the hot seat at the most critical time for the Group when decisions calibrated and ratified by the Group chairman were being executed by the only member of the board of directors who resides in India.

Seafood exports, the staple diet on which the Choice Group nourishes itself and looks upon for sustenance, is gradually being moved out of Kerala. A decision borne out of the fact that 100 per cent of the Choice Seafood raw material has been, for a while, sourced from outside Kerala, mostly from Andhra Pradesh.

The clincher was the runaway rise in the fuel cost, which has begun burning a hole in the profitability of operations at the Choice, Kochi factory. That has led to the first production line to be set up in Bapatla, a part of the famed Tenali region in Andhra Pradesh.

'In 2021, the transportation cost was bleeding us to the tune of ₹120 million a year, eating considerably into our operating profits. It was in mid-2021 that we shifted one production line from Kochi to Bapatla, near Vijayawada in West Godavari, where we have taken a seafood processing factory on lease. The production there comprises the uncooked exports,' points out Thomas about the rationale behind the relocation of production that is currently underway.

From a commercial perspective, a seafood exporting company like Choice with shrimp accounting for a major share, continuing in Kerala was no longer a viable proposition.

'Not with Andhra Pradesh and Tamil Nadu accounting for 100 per cent of our raw material. We have been planning this for some time but the pandemic has delayed the shifting. Since the aquaculture shrimp farms are right outside the Bapatla facility and the farmers just stroll in with their harvest, there are no trucks needed for transportation, unlike in the case of Kochi, which was costing us ₹10 million each month,' adds Thomas.

It is in this context that the seafood processing plant that is coming up in Andhra Pradesh with the Government of India funding assumes significance. There will be total synergy once the cooked products have a base along the East Godavari coastline, where the two facilities are located merely a couple of hours away.

Finally, the logistics are falling in place. Factor in the lag period between harvesting the shrimp and getting it processed at the Kochi facility and there is that aspect about the relative freshness of shrimp that gets exported to the US.

There was another interesting development in 2021—the recasting of the Choice Group's corporate identity with Chennai as its headquarters. The Choice Group, which already had its registered office for the past six years in the Kilpauk area along the Poonamalee High Road, has finally relocated its operational base to a building which has come up where the iconic Shanthi Theatre, owned by Sivaji Ganesan, was once located.

JT is convinced there is much to be gained by having his Indian operations based out of Chennai. The move was far from sudden as the Choice Group registered office was shifted there about five years ago.

The relocation plan gathered momentum with the acquisition of a second office space in the same building, to provide space for more staff. Both properties have been purchased outright, reinstating the company's resolve to be known as a Chennai-based company.

'Being a Kerala-based company has come at a cost and I thought it was high time we moved beyond our emotional ties with Kochi. With the acquisition of the second office, at 4,000 square feet which is as big as the first one, we have moved the entire team from Kochi. Our presence in Kerala will now be limited to the Choice Schools,' JT rationalizes his relocation plans.

Curiously, it is the Government of India, by choosing Choice to be a beneficiary of the Production Linked Incentive (PLI) Scheme, that has set the ball rolling for JT's IPO plans, which he was so close to pulling off in 1995, with Kotak Finance as the lead manager. Quite an irony since for all the decades he struggled to keep his many projects afloat, not once did he fall back on any government scheme to make ends meet.

In retrospect, it has been a slow grind since that massive meltdown following the Choice Air fiasco. When he finally goes for that IPO planned for 2025, there will be many conjectures about what Choice missed out in those three decades. Indeed, it will be redemption time for JT if he manages to pull off a successful public listing. That could well be the cornerstone of his legacy.

He has already set the ball rolling by making a move for his Choice Europe offices in two countries to begin with. Surprisingly, the countries are Italy and Austria. More specifically, the new destinations are going to be Vienna and Milan. London has been given a miss. This move will provide a long-pending closure for JT who suffered much the last time he pushed for Choice UK when he posted a number of his close relatives to start the London office.

'My premature attempt to start our London office in 1988 led to a huge pile-up of debt. My wife still reminds me of the tense period when we visited London to try and sort out the financial liabilities that some of my nephews created for me in the UK. The advice I received was that I could face legal consequences once I returned to India,' he recalls.

JT still remembers the day many decades ago, when he drove his hired car to Heathrow airport with his wife and three young children; there was an air of concern. He started giving instructions as to what all she had to do once they stepped out of the Madras airport. It was with great relief that he accosted his lawyer Venkiteswaran who was waiting for them at the airport. They proceeded directly to Hotel Trident where the lawyer went on to dispel most fears and apprehensions harboured by JT.

'During that period I was tempted by what many advised me should be considered a windfall gain. What happened was our shipping unit was signed on by a renowned multinational company to handle a consignment valued at £60,000 from London to India. I was already in my hometown when I received an excited call from one of the many relatives who were handling our London office that £6,00,000 had been mistakenly deposited into my account!' reminisces JT who underlines the impact of the London debt from the late-1980s lasted a good twelve years.

Apparently the money had been sitting unnoticed in the Choice Group's shipping account for a few weeks already. Much to the dismay of many in their London office who probably saw this as the one sure-fire solution to square off all outstanding debts, JT decided to return the money.

Now, a quarter century later, JT is sure it makes eminent sense to open shop in Europe. He explains, 'This is very much a part of the next phase of my plan. Many years ago, in the late-1980s, we did plan Choice UK as a venture that was pursued along with Choice US. We were never in a position then to expand our presence in multiple locations outside India. Now, we are. This time round, we are initially weighing entry options into Italy and Austria where I took both my sons on a reconnaissance visit as recently as June.'

The reason for looking at the continent is obvious. Unlike in the past when Europe literally started with London, the post-Brexit scenario holds out significant economic advantage for companies that set up shop in any of the mainland countries with road access to a number of EU affiliates. JT is aiming to minimize his add-on costs by way of transportation of frozen food.

While the Choice Group's future seems secure, a pet peeve for JT has been what his legacy could be. If this has remained an unfinished task, the primary reason for it is that JT felt compelled to redefine it many times in the past couple of years. That was in sync with the multiple benchmarks he tried to set, one after the other. As some proved to be too demanding, he had no option but to constantly tweak the blueprint, which could be best described as a work in progress, all the time.

26

LIVING A LEGACY

CAN ONE MEASURE JT'S LIFE WITH CONSERVATIVE TOOLS OF success and failure? What is his real claim to fame? Going by the yardstick of wealth, there are many in his hometown who are far richer than JT. Many have diversified their portfolios by tapping into public funds with perfectly timed IPOs—not so has been the case with JT.

As he went about pursuing his ultimate dream of starting a shipping line, he lost precious years that could have taken his seafood business to greater heights. He went chasing dreams, which in retrospect, were impossible ones, like the airlines project which exposed his company to a period of financial turbulence.

He has always had to diversify into unrelated fields—apart from his foray into the airlines sector, JT also ventured into education and construction. For the many successes he can lay claim too, there have been a number of failures along the way.

Therefore, how does one define his legacy? What is special about JT? What is his true achievement? What is that one character trait separating him from many other businessmen?

The last part of the question is the easiest one to answer—passion. Add to that resilience and grit, two sides of the same coin, and one gets a picture of the man who dared to live his dreams. The key to that, of course, was that he had no fear of failure. Whenever he failed, he would make a course correction and simply move on.

These experiences and this attitude are the reasons that JT could bring to the table a rare passion that is often not seen in the measured way business is conducted, where profits and profitability alone determine the intent to engage. He needed to internalize all these character traits because that was the only way the tenth son, otherwise forgotten, could emerge as the successful one, from among eleven siblings.

He keeps periodically asserting that his entire life journey has been about fulfilling a legacy. Growing up as the youngest son in a big family, he often struggled to even get a nod of acknowledgment from the one he revered the most—his father. Consequently, many monumental decisions he took right through his life ended up being supplications for approval from his late father. Some term his devotion as the extremity of spirituality. JT has always worn this character trait on his sleeve, like a badge of honour. The one tangible fallout of this obsession was that JT took on the role of the ultimate patriarch with a vengeance. He made it his mission to transform himself into the overarching banyan tree that his father once was for the Olassayil family.

This role was never thrust upon JT. On the contrary, it was a quest for him, one he pursued like a pilgrim seeking the Holy Grail. By wrenching the leadership position from his two elder brothers, it became clear that he revelled in the new role, with the tacit blessing of his mother, Annamma.

Thus began the saga of the youngest sibling turning patriarch of the family, where he personally groomed almost a dozen of his nephews in the rough and tumble of trade and commerce. There were nieces, too. Most of them were absorbed into Choice and personally groomed by JT. Rajan was his favourite but is no more. Most others have grown wings and flown away, some of them turning direct competitors. Each one of them learnt the ropes at Choice Group, leveraging JT's need to have trusted family members in positions of power, especially for overseas postings. He says he has only wished the best for all who sought him out.

'A good example is what my young protégé, Arvin Varghese, did with his life, after I brought him to the US. He grabbed the big opportunity that came his way. I would have done the same. What hurt me was the underhand way a few of my nephews went about their plans, keeping me completely in the dark while working for Choice in key positions. It also disappointed me that they felt compelled to challenge me,' says JT in all candour.

Perhaps that is why he went all out to keep his wife and children insulated from life's turbulences. Clearly, that is one thing he chose to do differently from his father.

'I would come to know of the many pressure-cooker situations only weeks after Jose faced them, long after the pressure had dissipated. That has been and continues to be his hallmark. He believes in taking care of his family the old-fashioned way. I still remember it was the day after Thomas's first birthday that we took off for the US. His main preoccupation was shipping as he had by then entered into a contract with Ceylon Shipping,' says his wife, Elizabeth.

For Elizabeth, the initial days in the US were quite a challenge as they were perpetually cash-strapped. There can be no argument that $8,000 was far from sufficient to either run a business or sustain a young family—young Jose was trying to do both!

'It was a small apartment that we first occupied in New York, from 1987 through 1989 when we returned for the delivery of Divya, our third child. Jose and he sank millions into Thames Shipping in the late-1980s but unlike the big Choice Air setback of 1995, we recovered from the Thames Shipping debacle as Hyundai Merchant Marine signed up as a client,' adds Elizabeth, remembering those early years when they kept Kochi as their base but would return every year for the mandatory two-month stay to keep their green card alive.

Just as recessionary fears rear their head the world over in 2023, there are many purists who will question the wisdom of JT's global expansion plans but traditional moves have never been among his strong suits. On the contrary, he has thrived by being bold and unconventional. All the more so as JT is driven by the belief that he is ready with his legacy, one that would have made his father proud.

From his heart, JT strongly believes his true legacy is the Choice School and the strong student community he has bequeathed to the society. From a truly business perspective, what he has built from scratch is a multi-product company with multiple geographical presence—in Asia and Europe, apart from the US and India.

It is not as if the job is done, the legacy fulfilled. What has been typical for JT all his life continues as he is forever ready for another adventure before he can pass on the baton and hang up his boots. So far, his life has been all about the fulfillment of a dream that began when a young boy gazed across the ocean in his hometown in Kochi and wondered what lay beyond. In a sense, he is still living it, day by day.

That is his true legacy.

EPILOGUE

WALTZ OF DEATH

JT HAS ALWAYS BEEN FASCINATED BY DEATH. HE CALLS IT the grand finale, the ultimate celebration. He thinks of it more as a farewell fit for the relentless young wanderer who paved his way in this world with honesty, integrity and righteousness. Fulfilling not just his dreams for Choice, but those of his father, too.

For a man who has always done his utmost for perfection, he trusts no one else to plan his final farewell but himself. He often speaks about how the celebrations should begin.

'The school will perhaps be closed for half a day, but not the full day. They must work. Nothing shall stop. The various business verticals would take a call on how they would be a part of this send-off party for their boss,' says JT.

His wish list of attendees of the must-attend event are those who had both criticized and envied him the most. There would, of course, be his very few true friends in attendance along with his family.

For someone who has celebrated the highs and lows of life with equal fervour, one final hurrah is a reasonable ask, he reiterates. Music, dance, drama and cocktails along with a spread of delicacies—he wants it all.

'Let the party begin,' he says, with a glint in his eye. Why, he has even identified the person who would be in charge of the event!

Jose, even after his transformation as JT, is clear about what he is all about, irrespective of how others see him and how he would like to be sent off: 'I am scared of being alone. I am afraid of not being fully understood. I passionately wish to hold aloft integrity as my armour as the Japanese do while engaging in trade. Because my character alone would be the flag draped over my coffin.'

He has always claimed he would spend his last days in Japan, that he would wish to lead his retired life in a Spartan way, out of a small apartment in the countryside, somewhere in the outskirts of Tokyo.

'One day, I will just pack up and go away and be with the people who I admire most, the Japanese. But before that, I want to relax a bit, start seeing the world. Though I have visited France and Italy over a hundred times, there are things I have not done. I want to see the Eiffel Tower, visit the Vatican. But all this does not mean I am retiring or that I have lost my ambition to take the Choice Group to greater heights,' he says.

Those who know him well, especially his family, look at his bucket list pretty often with a sense of bemusement. They even joke and say let's see if you will go to Vatican as a traveller or go there as a dreamer and build a business empire around the Vatican. Elizabeth, his wife, says, 'You can't predict what he does or will do. His vision has always been a result of him being a workaholic, and not driven by love for tourism!'

So, visiting the Eiffel Tower, the Vatican, and so on were never a priority for him. 'What do I get from seeing the Eiffel Tower? It is not as good as you can see on a postcard or Netflix. People seem to believe that visiting these attractions is the only important thing; surely, visiting places must hold more meaning,' says JT.

He always used to visualize and wonder about how death happens, how a person might feel when the heart stops beating and the breath leaves the body, and where does the soul go afterwards? It is as intriguing to him as is his next corporate manoeuvre. What a transformation for a boy who was caught on camera in his pre-teens, peeking furtively at the body of his uncle, fear written all over his face.

Now, he dreams about his own death. It has to be a peaceful one and not a violent end. He does not want to be gone consumed by flames in a plane crash, nor drown while sailing his yacht. He wants a natural death, a perfect death.

When he dreams of the day he will be detached from his body, this is what he sees—a crowd gathered in front of the home where he lays silently, possibly with a smile on his face. VIPs, Choice School students, parents, teachers, all line up to pay their respects, and then go on to partake in the meticulously planned grand celebration.

Amidst all this, a new kindergarten parent of his school walks in with her four-year-old child. As they get closer to where he lays in the well-orchestrated walkthrough, the child looks at him and asks, 'Who is this man?' The mother holds his hand tightly and says, 'This is JT, the man who lived a life that others could only dream of, one that is worth emulating. He transformed many lives.'

She was not only planning to enroll her child in JT's school but was counting on him mentoring her little one over the next few years. That was one transformation she now had to accept would never happen.

There would also be many others who speak of the departed as they often do. 'Some say he was a seafood exporter from Kochi, others say he was more, that he was in the shipping business. I also heard a few swear he was some big shot in America. There are a few who knew him as a builder of tall buildings. Some even say he was a celebrity chef and a drummer, that he had many film stars as his friends. It all seems a bit confusing as he cannot be so many things together,' says an autorickshaw driver near Parvana junction in Fort Kochi where his ancestral home used to be.

JT is convinced that posterity will remember him not for the businesses he ran in India and the US, not for the employment he provided to hundreds of people and by extension, having imparted livelihood to as many families, nor for the contacts he developed both in the business community and the upmarket society, but as an educator who transformed young lives.

The story of young Jose that began with his personality projections into Gillette Jose will not be complete minus the following sequel to his fantasy about his final journey into what lies beyond this world.

'I often dream of myself, seeking entry at the Pearly Gates. I am stopped by St Peter, who after checking the Book of Life, says I do not figure in the list. Immediately, I seek an audience with God,' narrates JT, with a deadpan face.

'God passes his decree in a booming voice: *Jose from Fort Kochi has done nothing worthy of a place in Paradise*. 'Completely taken aback, I start listing some of my good deeds but to no avail. Suddenly, I realize what could possibly have gone wrong,' he continues sotto voce in all seriousness.

'I start pleading with God to check the name of JT instead of Jose. He looks at me with a hearty laugh and says, *So, you are that Jose who transformed himself into JT! Okay, you are now on my list.* I could not believe what had just happened—God had admitted he had made a mistake,' concludes JT, with no trace of humour or any glint of mischief in his eyes.

For a person who wears a nonchalant demeanour about what others think of him, JT's elaborate visualization of what happens post his death presents quite an intriguing image. One could flag that as the alternate reality. Then again, can a man's entire life be defined by a few random thoughts he entertains about his death?

In retrospect, was this story all about Jose or JT? His fantasy about the dialogue with God clearly reveals his preferred protagonist in this battle of identities. It is a matter of amazement that even in the inner recesses of his mind he chose the cultivated character to be superior to the identity he had inherited. Nevertheless, there could be no JT without Jose.

Jose's metamorphosis into JT was as much a conscious decision as it was a matter of survival, though at some point it became an obsession. Now, nobody can tell these personas apart, or so he believes. As far as he is concerned, all that does not matter, as long as the story of Choice is heard loud and clear—in India, the US and soon in Europe and some parts of Asia.

That is the plan as of now—a plan that has been conceived as painstakingly and as impeccably as his personal farewell party.

ACKNOWLEDGEMENTS

Jeena, my life partner for almost thirty-three years, for still believing in me.

My son, Aaron, for humouring my many whims and fancies with fortitude.

My daughter, Anna, my staunch critic even while proofreading this book.

My daughter-in-law, Vanshika, for being a source of constant encouragement.

JT's son, Thomas Jose, for his hands-on effort to get this project completed.

ABOUT THE AUTHOR

Vinod Mathew is a known columnist and journalist with over three decades of experience with the Indian print media. He divided the first seventeen years of his career among three business publications: *The Economic Times, Business Today* and *Hindu BusinessLine*, and the next thirteen years between two national dailies where he was resident editor: *The Indian Express*, Pune, and *The New Indian Express*, Kerala.

Always a prolific writer, he has of late been a columnist with MoneyControl, News18.com, ThePrint and a few other news portals. He published a collection of his articles as a book titled *Simply* in 2017.

Vinod splits time between his home state, Kerala, and the US, where his daughter lives.